Afghan
TRADITIONS ™

Create a Timeless
Treasury of Over 50
Distinctive Afghans
Designed for All the
Times of Your Life

the Needlecraft Shop ™

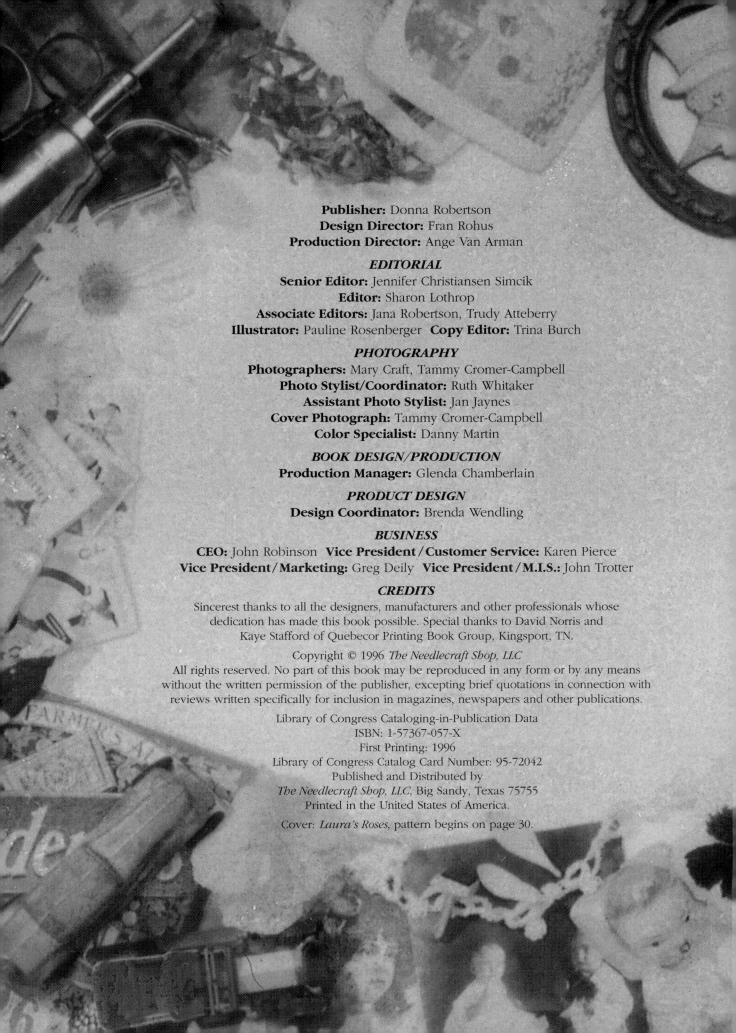

Publisher: Donna Robertson
Design Director: Fran Rohus
Production Director: Ange Van Arman

EDITORIAL
Senior Editor: Jennifer Christiansen Simcik
Editor: Sharon Lothrop
Associate Editors: Jana Robertson, Trudy Atteberry
Illustrator: Pauline Rosenberger **Copy Editor:** Trina Burch

PHOTOGRAPHY
Photographers: Mary Craft, Tammy Cromer-Campbell
Photo Stylist/Coordinator: Ruth Whitaker
Assistant Photo Stylist: Jan Jaynes
Cover Photograph: Tammy Cromer-Campbell
Color Specialist: Danny Martin

BOOK DESIGN/PRODUCTION
Production Manager: Glenda Chamberlain

PRODUCT DESIGN
Design Coordinator: Brenda Wendling

BUSINESS
CEO: John Robinson **Vice President/Customer Service:** Karen Pierce
Vice President/Marketing: Greg Deily **Vice President/M.I.S.:** John Trotter

CREDITS
Sincerest thanks to all the designers, manufacturers and other professionals whose
dedication has made this book possible. Special thanks to David Norris and
Kaye Stafford of Quebecor Printing Book Group, Kingsport, TN.

Library of Congress Cataloging-in-Publication Data
ISBN: 1-57367-057-X
First Printing: 1996
Library of Congress Catalog Card Number: 95-72042
Published and Distributed by
The Needlecraft Shop, LLC, Big Sandy, Texas 75755
Printed in the United States of America.

Cover: *Laura's Roses*, pattern begins on page 30.

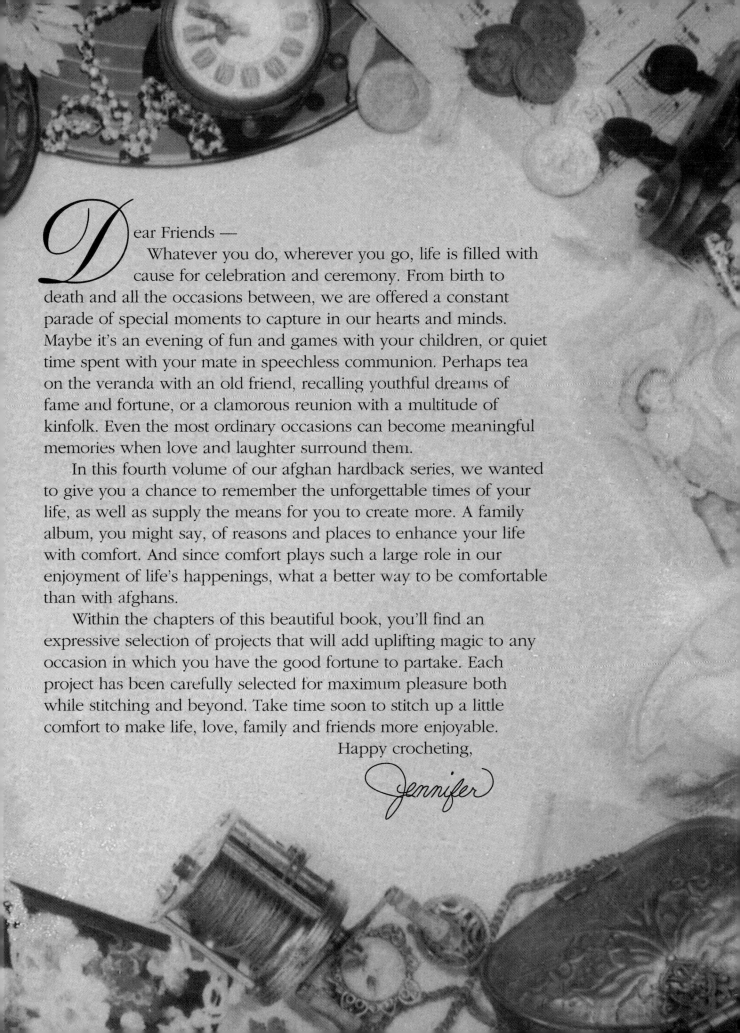

*D*ear Friends —

Whatever you do, wherever you go, life is filled with cause for celebration and ceremony. From birth to death and all the occasions between, we are offered a constant parade of special moments to capture in our hearts and minds. Maybe it's an evening of fun and games with your children, or quiet time spent with your mate in speechless communion. Perhaps tea on the veranda with an old friend, recalling youthful dreams of fame and fortune, or a clamorous reunion with a multitude of kinfolk. Even the most ordinary occasions can become meaningful memories when love and laughter surround them.

In this fourth volume of our afghan hardback series, we wanted to give you a chance to remember the unforgettable times of your life, as well as supply the means for you to create more. A family album, you might say, of reasons and places to enhance your life with comfort. And since comfort plays such a large role in our enjoyment of life's happenings, what a better way to be comfortable than with afghans.

Within the chapters of this beautiful book, you'll find an expressive selection of projects that will add uplifting magic to any occasion in which you have the good fortune to partake. Each project has been carefully selected for maximum pleasure both while stitching and beyond. Take time soon to stitch up a little comfort to make life, love, family and friends more enjoyable.

Happy crocheting,

Jennifer

TABLE OF *Contents*

CHAPTER 1
Back Porch Comforts

Patchwork Flowers   8
Velvet Morning   11
Sunlight & Shadows   12
Granny's Attic Window   17
Lazy Afternoon   19
Scalloped Squares   20

CHAPTER 2
Victorian Parlour

Champagne Lace   26
Laura's Roses   30
Cloisonñe   33
Burgundy Expressions   34
Blue Magic   36
Petite Medallions   39
Stars in the Mist   40

CHAPTER 3
Sun Room Splendor

Lavender Fascination   47
Wish Upon a Star   48
Spring Lattice   50
Sunflowers   53
Flower Fantasy   56
American Beauty   59

CHAPTER 4
Library Treasures

Cabled Lattice   64
Geometrix   67
Etched Copper   69
Plaited Ripple   70
Woven Fisherman   73
Circles, Checks & Squares   74

CHAPTER 5
Hospitality Suites

Lilac Time 80
Medley in Blue 83
Shifting Sapphires 85
Grapevine Lace 86
Rosewood Elegance 89
Vanilla Delight 90
Flight of Fancy 92

CHAPTER 6
Sweet Dreams Nursery

Quilted Pastels 99
Tender Innocence 100
New Baby on the Block 103
Panda Parade 107
Heavenly Rainbows 109
Bubbles & Broomsticks 110
Party Gingham 112

CHAPTER 7
Family Gatherings

Homespun Harmony 119
Touched by Color 121
Cranberry Frost 122
Jewels of Time 125
Southwest Echoes 126
Portrait of Santa 131
Treble-Toned Shells 132

CHAPTER 8
Bedroom Charm

Purple Passion 143
Christmas Snowflake 144
Diamonds & Ripples 147
Ruffles Galore 149
Colonial Charm 151
Bunches o' Blossoms 152

General Instructions

Getting Started 156
Stitch Guide 158
Acknowledgments 157
Index 160

Back Porch
Comforts

Patchwork Flowers

Cool summer nights, the old fishing hole, Sunday dinner at Grandma's — recall fond memories with this quilt-look classic.

Designed by
Mary Wilhelm

FINISHED SIZE
58" x 70".

MATERIALS
Worsted-weight yarn —
119 oz. assorted
colors, 43 oz. mint;
F crochet hook or
size needed to
obtain gauge.

GAUGE
Each Motif is 2" across.

SKILL LEVEL
Challenging

FIRST MOTIF

Rnd 1: With mint, for **front of Motif,** ch 4, 11 dc in 4th ch from hook, join with sl st in top of ch-3 (12 dc).

Rnd 2: Ch 3, dc in same st, 2 dc in each st around, join (24).

Rnd 3: For **back of Motif,** working this rnd in **back lps** only, ch 3, dc in each st around, join.

Rnd 4: Ch 3, skip next st, (dc in next st, skip next st) around, join, fasten off (12).

FIRST JOINED MOTIF

Rnds 1-2: With next color (see Assembly Diagram on page 15), repeat same rnds of First Motif.

NOTE: When **joining Motifs,** you will be working into the same lps on rnd 2 of last Motif made as dc sts of rnd 3 are worked into. Front lps on rnd 2 are left un-worked throughout.

Rnd 3: To **join Motifs,** ch 3; place front *(rnds 1 and 2)* of last Motif made on top of Motif you

are making with rnds 3 and 4 of last Motif made facing you, yo, insert hook through any *worked* **back lp** on rnd 2 of last Motif and through next *unworked* **back lp** of this Motif at same time, yo, complete as dc, (yo, insert hook through next **worked** back lp on rnd 2 of last Motif and next **unworked** back lp on this Motif at same time, yo, complete as dc) 2 times, dc in each **remaining back lp** on this Motif, join.

Rnd 4: Ch 3, skip next st, (dc in next st, skip next st) around, join, fasten off (12).

REMAINING MOTIFS (make 925)

Skipping one st between each group of 3 joined sts and joining on one, two or three sides as needed (see Motif Joining Diagram on page 15), work and join Motifs according to Assembly Diagram, using mint for back-ground and desired colors to form "flowers" as shown in photo.

Velvet Morning

As the first light dawns, grab your coffee and this lacy ripple, then enjoy a moment of meditation in thanks for life's simple pleasures.

AFGHAN

Row 1: With maroon, ch 176, dc in 4th ch from hook, dc in each of next 2 chs, *[(dc, ch 2, dc) in next ch, dc in next 4 chs], skip next 2 chs, dc in next 4 chs; repeat from * 14 more times; repeat between [ ], turn, fasten off (160 dc, 16 ch-2 sps).

Row 2: Join green with sc in 2nd st, ch 1, skip next st, sc in next st, ch 1, skip next st, *[(sc, ch 2, sc) in next ch sp, (ch 1, skip next st, sc in next st) 2 times], skip next 2 sts, (sc in next st, ch 1, skip next st) 2 times; repeat from * 14 more times; repeat between [ ] leaving last st unworked, turn.

Row 3: Sl st in first ch-1 sp, ch 4, dc in next ch-1 sp, ch 1, *[(dc, ch 2, dc) in next ch-2 sp, (ch 1, dc in next ch-1 sp) 2 times], skip next 2 sts, (dc in next ch-1 sp, ch 1) 2 times; repeat from * 14 more times; repeat between [ ] leaving last st unworked, turn.

Row 4: Sl st in first ch-1 sp, ch 1, sc in same sp, ch 1, sc in next ch-1 sp, ch 1, *[(sc, ch 2, sc) in next ch-2 sp, (ch 1, sc in next ch-1 sp) 2 times], skip next 2 sts, (sc in next ch-1 sp, ch 1) 2 times; repeat from * 14 more times; repeat between [ ] leaving last st unworked, turn, fasten off.

Row 5: Join maroon with sl st in first ch-1 sp, ch 3, dc in next st, dc in next ch-1 sp, dc in next st, *[(dc, ch 2, dc) in next ch-2 sp, (dc in next st, dc in next ch-1 sp) 2 times], skip next 2 sts, (dc in next ch-1 sp, dc in next st) 2 times; repeat from * 14 more times; repeat between [ ] leaving last st unworked, turn, fasten off.

Row 6: With dk. blue, repeat row 2, fasten off.

Row 7: Repeat row 5.

Rows 8-11: Repeat rows 2-5.

Row 12: With lt. blue, repeat row 2, fasten off.

Row 13: Repeat row 5.

Rows 14-119: Repeat rows 2-13 consecutively, ending with row 11. At end of last row, **do not** turn.

Rnd 120: Working around outer edge in sts and in ends of rows, join lt. blue with sc in 2nd st, ch 1, skip next st, sc in next st, ch 1, skip next st, *(sc, ch 2, sc) in next ch sp, (ch 1, skip next st, sc in next st) 2 times, skip next 2 sts, (sc in next st, ch 1, skip next st) 2 times; repeat from * 14 more times, (sc, ch 2, sc) in next ch sp, ch 1, skip next st, sc in next st, ch 1, skip next st, (sc, ch 2, sc) in next st, skip last st, ch 1, (sc in next row, ch 1) across; working in starting ch on opposite side of row 1, (sc, ch 2, sc) in first ch, ch 1, sc in next

Continued on page 14

Designed by
Katherine Eng

FINISHED SIZE
43" x 60".

MATERIALS
Worsted-weight yarn —
24 oz. maroon, 18 oz.
green, 5½ oz. lt. blue
and 5 oz. dk. blue;
G crochet hook or
is size needed to
obtain gauge.

GAUGE
4 dc = 1"; 4 dc rows and
4 sc rows = 3¾".

SKILL LEVEL
Average

Sunlight & Shadows

Create this striking ripple in red, off-white and dusky shades of blue to be your cozy companion for those lazy evenings on the patio.

Designed by
Katherine Eng

FINISHED SIZE
50" x 71"
not including Fringe.

MATERIALS
Worsted-weight yarn —
36 oz. off-white, 13 oz.
red, 5 oz. each lt. blue,
dk. blue, slate blue
and turquoise; G crochet
hook or size needed
to obtain gauge.

GAUGE
4 dc = 1"; 2 dc rows and
2 sc rows = 2".

SKILL LEVEL
Average

AFGHAN

Note: When joining next color or fastening off, leave a 7" end to be worked into Fringe.

Row 1: With off-white, ch 232, sc in 2nd ch from hook, sc in next ch, *[hdc in each of next 2 chs, dc in next ch, (2 dc, ch 2, 2 dc) next ch, dc in next ch, hdc in each of next 2 chs], sc in next 4 chs; repeat from * 19 more times; repeat between [ ], sc in each of last 2 chs, turn (294 sts, 21 ch sps).

Row 2: Sl st in next st, ch 1, sc in same st, ch 1, skip next st, (sc in next st, ch 1, skip next st) 2 times, *[(sc, ch 2, sc) in next ch sp, (ch 1, skip next st, sc in next st) 3 times], skip next 2 sts, (sc in next st, ch 1, skip next st) 3 times; repeat from * 19 more times; repeat between [ ] leaving last st unworked, turn, fasten off.

Row 3: Join dk. blue with sl st in first ch-1 sp, ch 4, (dc in next ch-1 sp, ch 1) 2 times, *[(dc, ch 2, dc) in next ch-2 sp, (ch 1, dc in next ch-1 sp) 3 times], skip next 2 sts, (dc in next ch-1 sp, ch 1) 3 times; repeat from * 19 more times; repeat between [ ] leaving last st unworked, turn, fasten off.

Row 4: Join red with sc in first ch-1 sp, ch 1, (sc in next ch-1 sp, ch 1) 2 times, *[(sc, ch 2, sc) in next ch-2 sp, (ch 1, sc in next ch-1 sp) 3 times], skip next 2 sts, (sc in next

ch-1 sp, ch 1) 3 times; repeat from * 19 more times; repeat between [ ] leaving last st unworked, turn, fasten off.

Row 5: Join off-white with sl st in first ch-1 sp, ch 3, dc in next st, (dc in next ch-1 sp, dc in next st) 2 times, *[(dc, ch 2, dc) in next ch-2 sp, (dc in next st, dc in next ch-1 sp) 3 times], skip next 2 sts, (dc in next ch-1 sp, dc in next st) 3 times; repeat from * 19 more times; repeat between [ ] leaving last st unworked, turn.

Rows 6-17: Repeat row 2-5 consecutively, working repeats of row 3 in color sequence of lt. blue, slate blue and turquoise.

Row 18: Repeat row 2, **do not** fasten off.

Row 19: Ch 3, dc in next st, (dc in next ch-1 sp, dc in next st) 2 times, *[(dc, ch 2, dc) in next ch-2 sp, (dc in next st, dc in next ch-1 sp) 3 times], skip next 2 sts, (dc in next ch-1 sp, dc in next st) 3 times; repeat from * 19 more times; repeat between [ ] leaving last st unworked, turn.

Rows 20-35: Repeat rows 2-5 consecutively, working repeats of row 3 in color sequence of turquoise, slate blue, lt. blue and dk. blue.

Row 36: Repeat row 2, **do not** fasten off.

Continued on page 14

Sunlight & Shadows

Continued from page 12

Row 37: Repeat row 19.

Rows 38-52: Repeat rows 2-5 consecutively, working repeats of row 3 in color sequence of dk. blue, lt. blue, slate blue and turquoise, ending with row 4. At end of last row, **do not** fasten off.

Row 53: Sl st in next ch-1 sp, ch 1, sc in same sp, ch 3, (sc in next ch-1 sp, ch 3) 2 times, *[(sc, ch 3, sc) in next ch-2 sp, (ch 3, sc in next ch-1 sp) 3 times], skip next 2 sts, (sc in next ch-1 sp, ch 3) 3 times; repeat from * 19 more times; repeat between [ ], **do not** turn, fasten off.

Row 54: Working in starting ch on opposite side of row 1, join off-white with sc in first ch, sc in next ch, *[hdc in each of next 2 chs, dc in next ch, (2 dc, ch 2, 2 dc) in next ch, dc in next ch, hdc in each of next 2 chs], sc in next 4 chs; repeat from * 19 more times; repeat between [ ], sc in each of last 2 chs, turn.

Rows 55-106: Repeat rows 2-53.

FRINGE

For **each Fringe,** cut three strands yarn each 14" long. With all strands held together, fold in half, insert hook in end of row, draw all loose ends and 7" tails at ends of rows through fold, tighten. Trim ends.

Matching row colors, Fringe in end of each sc row excluding last row on each side.

Velvet Morning

Continued from page 11

ch, ch 1, skip next ch, sc in next ch, skip next ch, [(sc in next ch, ch 1, skip next ch) 2 times, (sc, ch 2, sc) in next ch-2 sp, (ch 1, skip next ch, sc in next ch) 2 times, skip next ch]; repeat between [ ] 14 more times, sc in next ch, ch 1, skip next ch, sc in next ch, ch 1, (sc, ch 2, sc) in last ch, ch 1, (sc in next row, ch 1) across, sc in same st as first st, ch 2, join with sl st in first sc, fasten off.

Rnd 121: Join maroon with sl st in last st, ch 3, (2 dc, ch 2, 2 dc) in next corner ch-2 sp, dc in next st, (dc in next ch-1 sp, dc in next st) 2 times, (dc, ch 2, dc) in next ch-2 sp, [(dc in next st, dc in next ch-1 sp) 2 times, *skip next 2 sts, (dc in next ch-1 sp, dc in next st) 2 times, (dc, ch 2, dc) in next ch-2 sp, (dc in next st, dc in next ch-1 sp) 2 times; repeat from * 14 more times], dc in next st, (2 dc, ch 2, 2 dc) in next corner ch-2 sp, dc in each st and in each ch-1 sp across to next corner ch-2 sp, (2 dc, ch 2, 2 dc) in next corner ch-2 sp; repeat between [ ], skip next 2 sts, (dc in next ch-1 sp, dc in next st) 2 times, (2 dc, ch 2, 2 dc) in next corner ch-2 sp, dc in each st and in each ch-1 sp across, join with sl st in top of ch-3.

Rnd 122: Ch 3, skip next 2 sts, (sl st, ch 3, sl st) in next corner ch sp, ch 3, skip next 2 sts, (sl st in next st, ch 3, skip next 2 sts) 2 times, (sl st, ch 3, sl st) in next ch sp, *ch 3, skip next 2 sts, sl st in next st, ch 2, skip next st, sl st in each of next 2 sts, ch 3, skip next st, sl st in next st, ch 3, skip next 2 sts, (sl st, ch 3, sl st) in next ch sp; repeat from * 14 more times, ch 3, skip next 2 sts, (sl st in next st, ch 3, skip next 2 sts) 2 times, ◊(sl st, ch 3, sl st) in next corner ch sp, ch 3, skip next 2 sts, (sl st in next st, ch 3, skip next 2 sts) across◊ to next corner ch sp, (sl st, ch 3, sl st) in next corner ch sp, (ch 3, skip next 2 sts, sl st in next st) 2 times, [sl st in next st, ch 2, skip next st, sl st in next st, ch 3, skip next 2 sts, (sl st, ch 3, sl st) in next ch sp, ch 3, skip next 2 sts, sl st in next st, ch 2, skip next st, sl st in next st]; repeat between [ ] 14 more times, (sl st in next st, ch 3, skip next 2 sts) 2 times; repeat between ◊◊, join with sl st in joining sl st of last rnd, fasten off.

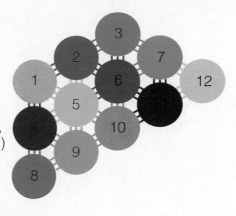

Patchwork Flowers

Instructions on page 8

MOTIF JOINING DIAGRAM
(Colors shown are for contrast only,
match color of Motif to joining lines.)

ASSEMBLY DIAGRAM
(Background Motifs are shown in lt. green;
flower colors are for placement only.)

Granny's Attic Window

Like sunlight splintered through a prism, this colorful variation of the traditional granny-square will brighten your home with rays of joy.

MOTIF (make 24 of each color)

Rnd 1: With darkest shade, ch 4, sl st in first ch to form ring, ch 3, 2 dc in ring, ch 1, (3 dc in ring, ch 1) 3 times, join with sl st in top of ch-3 (12 dc, 4 ch-1 sps).

Rnd 2: Sl st in each of next 2 sts, sl st in next ch sp, ch 3, 2 dc in same sp, ch 1, (3 dc, ch 1, 3 dc) in next ch sp, ch 1, 3 dc in next ch sp changing to med. shade in last st made *(see fig. 12, page 159)*, ch 1, 3 dc in same sp, ch 1, 3 dc in next ch sp changing to lt. shade in last st made, ch 1, 3 dc in same sp, ch 1, 3 dc in same sp as first st changing to dk. shade in last st made, ch 1, join (8 3-dc groups, 8 ch sps).

Rnd 3: Sl st in each of next 2 sts, sl st in next ch sp, ch 3, 2 dc in same sp, ch 1, (3 dc, ch 1, 3 dc) in next ch sp, ch 1, 3 dc in next ch sp changing to med. shade in last st made, ch 1, (3 dc, ch 1, 3 dc) in next ch sp, ch 1, 3 dc in next ch sp, ch 1, 3 dc in next ch sp changing to lt. shade in last st made, ch 1, 3 dc in same sp, ch 1, 3 dc in next ch sp, ch 1, (3 dc, ch 1, 3 dc) in next ch sp changing to dk. shade in last st made, ch 1, join (12 3-dc groups, 12 ch sps).

Rnd 4: Sl st in each of next 2 sts, sl st in next ch sp, ch 3, 2 dc in same sp, ch 1, (3 dc, ch 1, 3 dc) in next ch sp, (ch 1, 3 dc in next ch sp) 2 times changing to med. shade in last st made, ch 1, (3 dc, ch 1, 3 dc) in next ch sp, (ch 1, 3 dc in next ch sp) 3 times changing to lt. shade in last st made, ch 1, 3 dc in same ch sp as last st made, ch 1, (3 dc in next ch sp, ch 1) 2 times, (3 dc, ch 1, 3 dc) in next ch sp changing to dk. shade in last st made, ch 1, 3 dc in next ch sp, ch 1, join, fasten off (16 3-dc groups, 16 ch sps).

Holding Motifs right sides together, matching sts, working through both thicknesses with matching colors, sl st together through **front lps** only according to Assembly Diagram on page 23.

BORDER

Notes: For **beginning V-stitch (beg V-st),** ch 4, dc in same sp.

For **V-stitch (V-st),** (dc, ch 1, dc) in next ch sp.

Rnd 1: Working around outer edge, join black with sl st in any corner ch sp, beg V-st, ch 2, V-st in same sp, *[ch 1, (V-st in next ch sp, ch 1) across] to next corner ch sp,

Designed by
Kathleen Stuart

FINISHED SIZE
47" square.

MATERIALS
Worsted-weight yarn —
4 oz. black, 4 oz. each
of three shades of
green, blue, purple,
rose, orange and
yellow; F crochet
hook or size needed
to obtain gauge.

GAUGE
Motif is 3¾" square.

SKILL LEVEL
Average

Continued on page 23

Lazy Afternoon

Enjoy restful relaxation with the fruits of your labor when you stitch this delightfully easy one-piece design in muted floral tones.

AFGHAN

Note: For **shell,** (2 dc, ch 2, 2 dc) in next ch sp.

Rnd 1: With lt. mint, ch 6, sl st in first ch to form ring, ch 3, 2 dc in ring, ch 2, (3 dc in ring, ch 2) 3 times, join with sl st in top of ch-3 (12 dc, 4 ch sps).

Rnds 2-3: Ch 3, dc in each st around with shell in each ch sp, join, ending with 11 dc between corner ch sps on last rnd. At end of last rnd, fasten off.

Rnd 4: Join lt. blue with sl st in any st, ch 3, dc in each st around with shell in each ch sp, join.

Rnds 5-7: Repeat rnd 2. At end of last rnd, fasten off.

Rnd 8: With lt. rose, repeat rnd 4.

Rnds 9-12: Repeat rnd 2. At end of last rnd, fasten off.

Rnd 13: With lilac, repeat rnd 4.

Rnds 14-18: Repeat rnd 2. At end of last rnd, fasten off.

Rnd 19: With dk. mint, repeat rnd 4, fasten off (75 dc between corner ch sps).

Notes: For **beginning shell (beg shell),** ch 3, (dc, ch 3, 2 dc) in same sp.

For **popcorn (pc),** 4 dc in next st, drop lp from hook, insert hook in first st of 4-dc group, pick up dropped lp, draw through st.

Rnd 20: Join lt. mint with sl st in any ch sp, beg shell, *[ch 1, skip next st, (pc in next st, ch 1, skip next st) across] to next corner ch sp, shell in corner ch sp; repeat from * 2 more times; repeat between [ ], join, fasten off.

Rnd 21: Join dk. mint with sl st in any corner ch-2 sp, beg shell, dc in each st and in each ch-1 sp around with shell in each corner ch-2 sp, join, fasten off.

Rnd 22: With lt. blue, repeat rnd 4.

Rnd 23: Repeat rnd 2, fasten off.

Rnd 24: With lt. rose, repeat rnd 4, fasten off.

Rnd 25: With lilac, repeat rnd 4, fasten off.

Rnd 26: With yellow, repeat rnd 4, fasten off.

Rnd 27: Join lt. rose with sl st in any corner ch sp, ch 3, dc in same sp, dc in each st across to next corner ch sp, 2 dc in next ch sp changing to lilac in last st made *(see fig. 12, page 159)*, ch 3, 2 dc in same sp, dc in each st across to next corner ch sp, 2 dc in next ch sp changing to lt. blue in last st made, ch 3, 2 dc in same sp, dc in each st across to next corner ch sp, 2 dc in next ch sp changing to lt. mint in last st made, ch 3, 2 dc in same sp, dc in each st across, 2 dc in same sp as first st, ch 3, join, fasten off.

Rnd 28: With gray, repeat rnd 4.

Continued on page 22

Designed by
Fran Hetchler

FINISHED SIZE
57" square.

MATERIALS
Worsted-weight yarn —
10 oz. each lt. mint,
lt. blue, lt. rose and lilac,
5 oz. each lt. gray, yellow, dk. mint, dk. blue
and dk. rose;
H crochet hook or
size needed to
obtain gauge.

GAUGE
7 dc = 2";
11 dc rnds = 6".

SKILL LEVEL
Easy

Scalloped Squares

Lacy strips and multicolored squares set patchwork-style among blocks of rose, green and blue form a charming quilt-look throw.

Designed by
Dorothy C. Myers

FINISHED SIZE
68" square.

MATERIALS
Worsted-weight yarn —
22 oz. white, 13 oz.
blue, 11 oz. each rose
and mint, 7 oz.
variegated; tapestry
needle; H crochet
hook or size needed
to obtain gauge.

GAUGE
7 dc = 2"; Rnds 1-2 of
Square = 3" across.

SKILL LEVEL
Average

LARGE MOTIF (make 6 blue, 5 mint and 5 rose)

Rnd 1: With color, ch 3, sl st in first ch to form ring, ch 3, 2 dc in ring, ch 2, (3 dc in ring, ch 2) 3 times, join with sl st in top of ch-3 (12 dc, 4 ch sps).

Rnds 2-3: Ch 3, dc in each st around with (2 dc, ch 2, 2 dc) in each ch sp, join, ending with 44 dc and 4 ch sps in last rnd. At end of last rnd, fasten off.

Rnd 4: Join white with sc in any ch sp, *[skip next 2 sts, 7 dc in next st, skip next 2 sts, sc in next st, skip next 2 sts, 7 dc in next st, skip next 2 sts], 2 sc in next ch sp; repeat from * 2 more times; repeat between [ ], sc in same sp as first st, join with sl st in first sc (68 sts).

Rnd 5: Ch 1, sc in first st, *[sc in next 4 sts, skip next 3 sts, 9 dc in next sc, skip next 3 sts], sc in next 6 sts; repeat from * 2 more times; repeat between [ ], sc in last 5 sts, join.

Rnd 6: Ch 3, dc in next 8 sts, *[(2 dc, ch 2, 2 dc) in next st], dc in next 18 sts; repeat from * 2 more times; repeat between [ ], dc in last 9 sts, join with sl st in top of ch-3.

Rnd 7: Ch 3, dc in each of next 2 sts, [*ch 1, dc in next 7 sts, ch 1, dc in next st, (2 dc, ch 2, 2 dc) in next ch sp, dc in next st, ch 1, dc in next 7 sts, ch 1], dc in next 6 sts; repeat from * 2 more times; repeat

between [ ], dc in each of last 3 sts, join, fasten off.

Rnd 8: Join same color as rnd 1 with sc in any corner ch-2 sp, *[7 tr in next ch-1 sp, (skip next 3 sts, sc in next st, 7 tr in next ch-1 sp) 3 times], sc in next ch-2 sp; repeat from * 2 more times; repeat between [ ], join with sl st in first sc, fasten off.

Row 9: Working in rows; for **first point,** join same color with sc in 4th tr of first 7-tr group, (7 tr in next sc, sc in 4th tr of next 7-tr group) 3 times leaving remaining sts unworked, turn.

Row 10: Sl st in next 4 sts, ch 1, sc in same st as last sl st, (7 tr in next sc, sc in 4th tr of next 7-tr group) 2 times leaving remaining sts unworked, turn.

Row 11: Sl st in next 4 sts, ch 1, sc in same st as last sl st, 9 tr in next sc, sc in 4th tr of last 7-tr group leaving remaining sts unworked, **do not** turn, fasten off.

Row 9: For **next point,** join same color with sc in 4th tr of next 7-tr group on rnd 8, (7 tr in next sc, sc in 4th tr of next 7-tr group) 3 times leaving remaining sts unworked, turn.

Rows 10-11: Repeat same rows of first point.

Rows 9-11: For **remaining points,** repeat next point two

Continued on page 22

Scalloped Squares

Continued from page 20

more times for a total of four points. At end of last row on last point, **do not** fasten off.

Rnd 12: Working around outer edge, ch 1, sc in first st, *[(sc in each of next 3 tr, sc in next sc) across to 9-tr group on next corner, sc in next 4 tr; for **corner,** 3 sc in next tr; sc in next 4 tr], sc in next sc; repeat from * 2 more times; repeat between [ ], join with sl st in first sc, fasten off (35 sc between each corner sc).

SMALL SQUARE (make 25)

Rnds 1-2: With variegated, repeat same rnds of Large Square, ending with 28 dc and 4 ch sps in last rnd.

Rnd 3: Ch 1, sc in each st around with 5 sc in each ch sp, join with sl st in first sc, fasten off (11 sc between each corner sc).

STRIP (make 40)

Row 1: With white, ch 43, dc in 4th ch from hook, dc in each ch across, turn (41 dc).

Row 2: Ch 4, skip next st, dc in next st, (ch 1, skip next st, dc in next st) across, turn.

Row 3: Ch 1, sc in each st and in each ch sp across, turn.

Row 4: Repeat row 2.

Row 5: Ch 3, dc in each st and in each ch

sp across, fasten off.

Easing to fit, sew all pieces together according to Assembly Diagram.

BORDER

Rnd 1: Working around entire outer edge, join variegated with sc in any st, sc in each st and in each seam around with 3 sc in each corner ch sp, join with sl st in first sc.

Rnds 2-3: Ch 1, sc in each st around with 3 sc in each center corner st, join. At end of last rnd, fasten off.

ASSEMBLY DIAGRAM

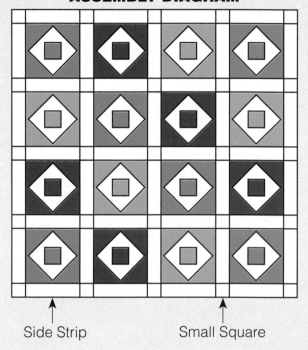

Side Strip   Small Square

Lazy Afternoon

Continued from page 19

Rnd 29: Repeat rnd 2, fasten off.

Rnd 30: With dk. blue, repeat rnd 4, fasten off.

Rnd 31: With lt. blue, repeat rnd 20.

Rnd 32: With dk. blue, repeat rnd 21.

Rnd 33: With lt. mint, repeat rnd 4.

Rnds 34-35: Repeat rnd 2. At end of last rnd, fasten off.

Rnd 36: With lt. blue, repeat rnd 4.

Rnds 37-39: Repeat rnd 2. At end of last rnd, fasten off.

Rnd 40: With gray, repeat rnd 4.

Rnd 41: Repeat rnd 2, fasten off.

Rnd 42: With dk. rose, repeat rnd 4, fasten off.

Rnd 43: With lt. rose, repeat rnd 20.

Rnd 44: With dk. rose, repeat rnd 21.

Rnd 45: With yellow, repeat rnd 4, fasten off.

Rnd 46: Join lt. mint with sl st in any cor-

Granny's Attic Window
Continued from page 17

(V-st, ch 2, V-st) in next ch sp; repeat from *
2 more times; repeat between [ ], join with sl

st in 3rd ch of ch-4.

Rnds 2-3: Sl st in next ch sp, sl st in next st, sl st in next ch sp, beg V-st, ch 2, V-st in same sp, *[skip next ch sp, (V-st in next ch sp, skip next ch sp) across] to next corner ch-2 sp, (V-st, ch 2, V-st) in next ch-2 sp; repeat from * 2 more times; repeat between [ ], join. At end of last rnd, fasten off.

ASSEMBLY DIAGRAM

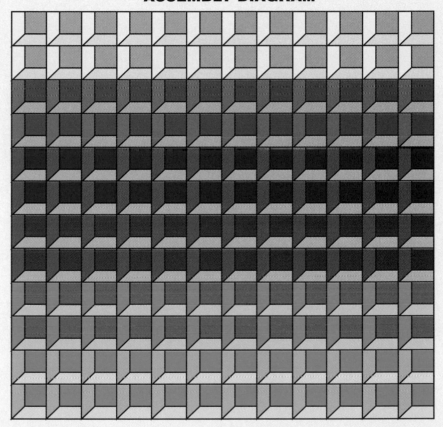

ner ch sp, ch 3, dc in same sp, dc in each st across to next corner ch sp, 2 dc in next ch sp changing to lt. blue in last st made, ch 3, 2 dc in same sp, dc in each st across to next corner ch sp, 2 dc in next ch sp changing to lilac in last st made, ch 3, 2 dc in same sp, dc in each st across to next corner ch sp, 2 dc in next ch sp changing to lt. rose in last st made, ch 3, 2 dc in same sp, dc in each st across, 2 dc in same sp as first st, ch 3, join, fasten off.

Rnd 47: With gray, repeat rnd 4, fasten off.

Rnd 48: With lilac, repeat rnd 4.

Rnds 49-51: Repeat rnd 2, ending with 203 dc between corner ch sps in last rnd. At end of last rnd, fasten off.

Rnd 52: Join dk. mint with sl st in any ch sp, ch 3, 4 dc in same sp, *[skip next st, sc in next st, skip next st, (5 dc in next st, skip next st, sc in next st, skip next st) across] to next ch sp, 5 dc in next ch sp; repeat from * 2 more times; repeat between [ ], join, fasten off.

Victorian
Parlour

Champagne Lace

Imbued with elegance and graceful charm, this artful masterpiece will enrich your decor with the lavish look of antique lace.

Designed by
Rena V. Stevens

FINISHED SIZE
52" x 74"
not including Fringe.

MATERIALS
Worsted-weight yarn —
49 oz. white, 10½ oz.
each lt. beige and dk.
beige; tapestry needle;
H crochet hook or size
needed to obtain gauge.

GAUGE
7 dc sts = 2";
2 dc rows = 1".

SKILL LEVEL
Average

CENTER PANEL
Center Strip

Row 1: With white, ch 368, sc in 2nd ch from hook, *skip next 2 chs, (dc, ch 2, dc) in next ch, skip next 2 chs, sc in next ch; repeat from * across, turn (122 dc, 62 sc).

Row 2: Ch 5, dc in first st, *sc in next ch-2 sp, (dc, ch 2, dc) in **front lp** of next sc; repeat from * across, turn.

Row 3: Sl st in next ch sp, ch 1, sc in same sp, *(dc, ch 2, dc) in **front lp** of next sc, sc in next ch-2 sp; repeat from * across, turn.

Rows 4-53: Repeat rows 2 and 3 alternately.

Row 54: Ch 1, sc in first st, (ch 1, sc in next ch sp, ch 1, sc in next sc) across, turn, fasten off (245 sts and chs).

Row 55: Join dk. beige with sc in first st, sc in next 10 sts and chs, skip next st or ch, (sc in next 11 sts or chs, skip next st or ch) 19 times, sc in each of next 3 sts and chs, skip next st or ch, sc in last st, **do not** turn, fasten off (224 sc).

Row 56: Join white with sl st in first st, ch 3, dc in each st across, **do not** turn, drop white.

Note: For **picot**, ch 3, sl st in 3rd ch from hook.

Row 57: Working this row in **front lps** only, join lt. beige with sl st in first st, *skip next 2 sts; for **lace scallop,** (dc, picot, dc, picot, dc,

picot, dc) in next st; skip next 2 sts, sc in next st; repeat from * across to last st, sl st in last st, turn, fasten off.

Row 58: Working in both lps of unworked sts and in remaining lps of worked sts on row 56, pick up white, ch 3, dc in each st across, turn (224 dc).

Row 59: Ch 3, dc in each st across, turn.

Row 60: Ch 3, dc in each of next 3 sts, dc in next st and center picot of next lace scallop on row 57 at same time, (dc in next 5 sts, dc in next st and center picot of next lace scallop on row 57 at same time) 36 times, dc in each of last 3 sts, drop white, turn.

Row 61: Working this row in **front lps** only, join dk. beige with sl st in first st, *sl st in next st, ch 1, sl st in next st, ch 3, skip next 4 sts, (dc, ch 3, dc) in next st, ch 3, skip next 4 sts; repeat from * 19 more times, sl st in next st, ch 1, sl st in each of last 2 sts, turn.

Row 62: Sl st in next st, ch 1, *sc in next ch-1 sp, ch 3, skip next ch-3 sp, (dc, ch 2) 4 times in next ch-3 sp, dc in same sp as last dc, ch 3, skip next ch-3 sp; repeat from * 19 more times, sc in last ch-1 sp, ch 1, sl st in last sl st, turn.

Row 63: Ch 1, sl st in next ch-1 sp, *ch 1, (sl st, ch 1, sl st) in next ch-3 sp, (ch 4, sl st in next ch-2

Continued on page 28

Champagne Lace
Continued from page 26

sp) 4 times, ch 4, (sl st, ch 1, sl st) in next ch-3 sp; repeat from * 19 more times, ch 3, sl st in last sl st, **do not** turn, fasten off.

Row 64: Working in both lps of unworked sts and in remaining lps of worked sts on row 60, pick up white, ch 3, dc in each st across, turn (224 dc).

Rows 65-67: Ch 3, dc in each st across, turn.

Row 68: Ch 3, dc in next 6 sts, dc in next st and center **back lp** of next lace scallop at same time, (dc in next 10 sts, dc in next st and center **back lp** of next lace scallop at same time) 19 times, dc in last 7 sts, turn.

Row 69: Ch 3, dc in each st across, drop white, turn.

Row 70: Working this row in **front lps** only, join lt. beige with sl st in first st, ch 4, skip next 2 sts, *sl st in next st, ch 1, sl st in next st, skip next 3 sts, (tr, ch 3) 4 times in next st, tr in same st as last tr, skip next 3 sts; repeat from * 23 more times, sl st in next st, ch 1, sl st in next st, ch 2, dc in last st, turn.

Row 71: Ch 2, *(tr, ch 3, tr) in next ch-1 sp, ch 3, skip next ch-3 sp, (sl st in next ch-3 sp, ch 3) 2 times, skip next ch-3 sp; repeat from * 23 more times, (tr, ch 3, tr) in next ch-1 sp, ch 1, dc in last ch sp, turn.

Row 72: Sl st in next ch-1 sp, ch 1, *(sc, ch 1, sc) in next ch-3 sp, ch 2, skip next ch-3 sp, (tr, picot) 3 times in next ch-3 sp, tr in same ch sp as last tr, ch 2, skip next ch-3 sp; repeat from * 23 more times, (sc, ch 1, sc) in next ch-3 sp, ch 1, sl st in last ch-2 sp, **do not** turn, fasten off.

Row 73: Working in both lps of unworked sts and in remaining lps of worked sts on row 69, pick up white, ch 3, dc in each st across, turn (224 dc).

Rows 74-77: Ch 3, dc in each st across, turn.

Row 78: Ch 3, dc in next 7 sts, dc in next st and **back lp** of center picot on next lace scallop at same time, (dc in next 8 sts, dc in next st and **back lp** of center picot on next lace scallop at same time) 23 times, dc in last 8 sts, turn.

Rows 79-80: Ch 3, dc in each st across, turn. At end of last row, drop white.

Row 81: Working this row in **front lps** only, join lt. beige with sl st in first st, sl st in next st, ch 5, skip next 2 sts, *(sc in next st, ch 5, skip next 2 sts) 2 times, sc in next st, ch 3, skip next 3 sts, (2 dc in next st, ch 3) 2 times, skip next 3 sts; repeat from * 13 more times, (sc in next st, ch 5, skip next 2 sts) 2 times, sc in next st, ch 5, skip next 2 sts, sc in last st, turn.

Row 82: Ch 2, sl st in first ch-5 sp, ch 4, (sc in next ch-5 sp, ch 5, sc in next ch-5 sp, ch 3, skip next ch-3 sp, dc in each of next 2 sts, ch 7, skip next ch-3 sp, dc in each of next 2 sts, ch 3, skip next ch-3 sp) 14 times, sc in next ch-5 sp, ch 5, sc in next ch-5 sp, ch 4, sl st in last ch sp, turn.

Row 83: Ch 2, sc in first ch-4 sp, ch 5, *sc in next ch-5 sp, ch 3, skip next ch-3 sp, dc in each of next 2 sts, ch 2, (tr, ch 1) 5 times in next ch-7 sp, tr in same sp as last tr, ch 2, dc in each of next 2 sts, ch 3, skip next ch-3 sp; repeat from * 13 more times, sc in next ch-5 sp, ch 5, sc in next ch-4 sp, tr in last ch-2 sp, turn.

Row 84: Sl st in first ch-5 sp, picot, *sl st in next sc, ch 3, skip next ch-3 sp, dc in each of next 2 sts, (picot, dc in next tr) 6 times, picot, dc in each of next 2 sts, ch 3, skip next ch-3 sp; repeat from * 13 more times, sl st in next sc, picot, sl st in next ch-5 sp, ch 2, sl st in last ch-2 sp, turn, fasten off.

Row 85: Working in both lps of unworked sts and in remaining lps of worked sts on row 80, pick up white, ch 3, dc in each st across, turn (224 dc).

Rows 86-91: Ch 3, dc in each st across, turn.

Row 92: Ch 3, dc in next 13 sts, dc in next st and **back lp** of center picot on next lace scallop at same time, (dc in next 14 sts, dc in next st and **back lp** of center picot on next lace scallop at same time) 13 times, dc in last 14 sts, turn.

Row 93: Ch 3, dc in each st across, turn, fasten off.

Row 94: Join dk. beige with sc in first st, sc in each st across, turn.

Row 95: Working this row in **front lps** only, ch 1, sc in first st, skip next 2 sts, (dc, picot, dc, picot, dc, picot, dc) in next st, skip next 3 sts,

*sc in next st, skip next 3 sts, (dc, picot, dc, picot, dc, picot, dc) in next st, skip next 3 sts; repeat from * across to last st, sc in last st, fasten off.

Row 96: Working in starting ch on opposite side of row 1, join white with sc in first ch, (ch 1, sc in ch at base of next 2 dc, ch 1, sc in ch at base of next sc) across, turn, fasten off (245 ch and sc).

Rows 97-137: Repeat rows 55-95.

FLOWER NO. 1 (make 2)

Rnd 1: With dk. beige, ch 6, sl st in first ch to form ring; for **petals,** (ch 2, 4 dc, ch 1, sl st) 4 times in ring (4 petals).

Rnd 2: (Ch 3, sl st in ring between 2nd and 3rd dc of next petal, ch 3, sl st in ring between 4th dc and sl st of same petal) 3 times, ch 3, sl st in ring between 2nd and 3rd dc of next petal, ch 3, sl st in last sl st of same petal (8 ch sps).

Rnd 3: (Ch 5, 4 tr, ch 2, sl st) in each ch sp around.

Rnd 4: Ch 1, (sl st in ch sp between 2nd and 3rd tr of next petal, ch 3) around, join with sl st in first sl st.

Rnd 5: (Ch 5, 6 tr, ch 2, sl st) in each ch sp around, fasten off.

FLOWER NO. 2 (make 6)

Rnds 1-3: With lt. beige, repeat same rnds of Flower No. 1. At end of last rnd, fasten off.

FLOWER NO. 3 (make 2)

Rnd 1: With dk. beige, ch 4, sl st in first ch to form ring; for **petals,** (ch 2, hdc, ch 1, sl st) 5 times in ring (5 petals).

Rnd 2: (Sl st in ring between ch-2 and hdc on next petal, ch 2) around, sl st in last sl st on last petal.

Rnd 3: (Ch 4, 5 dc, ch 1, sl st) in each ch sp around, fasten off.

FLOWER NO. 4 (make 2)

Rnd 1: With lt. beige, ch 5, sl st in first ch to form ring, (ch 4, sl st in ring) 5 times (5 ch sps).

Rnd 2: Working in ring through next ch sp, (sl st, ch 2, 2 dc, ch 1, sl st, ch 2) in ring; *working in ring through next ch sp, (2 dc, ch 1, sl st, ch 2) in ring; repeat from * 2 more times; working in ring through last ch sp, (2 dc, ch 1, sl st) in ring, join with sl st in first sl st, fasten off.

FLOWER NO. 5 (make 2)

With dk. beige, ch 4, sl st in first ch to form ring, (ch 2, 2 dc, ch 1, sl st) 4 times in ring, ch 2, 2 dc in ring, ch 1, join with sl st in first ch of first ch-2, fasten off.

FLOWER NO. 6 (make 2)

With lt. beige, ch 4, sl st in first ch to form ring, (ch 1, hdc, ch 3, sl st) 5 times in ring, fasten off.

Sew half of Flowers to left-hand side on one end of center section on Afghan according to Placement Diagram. With dk. beige, using Chain Stitch, embroider scroll lines.

Repeat on opposite end.

FRINGE

For **each Fringe,** cut 8 strands each 20" long. With all strands held together, fold in half, insert hook in row, draw fold through, draw all loose ends through fold, tighten. Trim ends.

With white and with matching colors at ends of lace and colored rows, Fringe every other row on each end of Afghan.

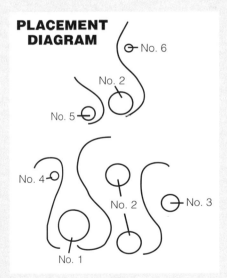

PLACEMENT DIAGRAM

No. 6
No. 2
No. 5
No. 4
No. 2
No. 3
No. 1

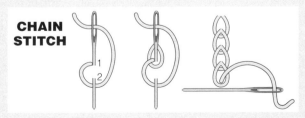

CHAIN STITCH

Laura's Roses

Satisfy your passion for uncommonly beautiful appointments with this exquisite creation suffused by the essecence of true Victoriana.

Designed by
Jennifer
Christiansen Simcik

FINISHED SIZE
46¾" x 59¼".

MATERIALS
Worsted-weight yarn —
21 oz. each black and
mauve, 17 oz. dk. rose
and 4 oz. soft pink;
tapestry needle;
G crochet hook or size
needed to obtain gauge.

GAUGE
Rnds 1-2 = 1¾" across.
Each Block is 6¼"
square.

SKILL LEVEL
Advanced

BLOCK (make 63)

Rnd 1: With soft pink, ch 2, 8 sc in 2nd ch from hook, join with sl st in first sc (8 sc).

Note: For **berry stitch (bs),** insert hook in next st, yo, draw lp through; working through first lp only, ch 3, yo, draw through both lps on hook.

Rnd 2: Ch 1, sc in first st, bs in same st, (sc, bs) in each st around, join, fasten off (8 sc, 8 bs).

Rnd 3: Join mauve with sl st in first st, ch 3, skip next st, (sl st in next st, ch 3, skip next st) around, join with sl st in first sl st (8 ch-3 sps).

Rnd 4: Sl st in first ch sp, ch 1, (sc, ch 2, sc) in same sp, ch 2, *(sc, ch 2, sc) in next ch sp, ch 2; repeat from * around, join with sl st in first sc (16 ch-2 sps).

Rnd 5: Sl st in first ch sp, ch 1, (sc, ch 3, sc, ch 3, sc) in same sp, ch 3, skip next ch sp, *(sc, ch 3, sc, ch 3, sc) in next ch sp, ch 3, skip next ch sp; repeat from * around, join, fasten off.

Rnd 6: Working behind rnd 5, in skipped ch sps of rnd 4, join dk. rose with sc in any ch sp, ch 3, sc in same sp, ch 3, *(sc, ch 3, sc) in next ch sp, ch 3; repeat from * around, join.

Rnd 7: Sl st in first ch sp, ch 1, (sc, ch 3, sc, ch 5, sc, ch 3, sc) in same sp, ch 2, skip next ch sp,

*(sc, ch 3, sc, ch 5, sc, ch 3, sc) in next ch sp, ch 2, skip next ch sp; repeat from * around, join.

Rnd 8: Ch 1; *working from back to front through next ch sp on rnd 6, dc around adjacent ch-3 sp on rnd 5, ch 2, sc over next ch sps on last 2 rnds, ch 2; repeat from * around, join with sl st in first dc, fasten off (8 dc, 8 sc, 16 ch-2 sps).

Rnd 9: Join black with sl st in first ch sp, ch 3, (dc, ch 2, 2 dc) in same sp, *[(dc, hdc, sc) in next ch sp, 3 sc in next ch sp, (sc, hdc, dc) in next ch sp], (2 dc, ch 2, 2 dc) in next ch sp; repeat from * 2 more times; repeat between [ ], join with sl st in top of ch-3 (52 sts, 4 ch-2 sps).

Rnd 10: Ch 1, sc in each st around with (sc, ch 2, sc) in each corner ch sp, join with sl st in first sc (15 sc on each edge between corner ch sps).

Rnd 11: Sl st in next st, ch 1, sc in same st, ch 1, skip next st, *(sc, ch 2, sc) in next corner ch sp, ch 1, skip next st, (sc in next st, ch 1, skip next st) across to next corner; repeat from * around, join, fasten off.

Rnd 12: Join mauve with sc in any corner ch sp, (sc, ch 2, 2 sc) in same sp, 2 sc in each ch-1 sp across to next corner ch sp, *(2 sc, ch 2, 2 sc) in next corner ch sp, 2 sc in each ch-1 sp across to next corner ch sp; repeat from * around,

Continued on page 42

Cloisonñe

Rich enamel-look squares of jeweltone colors framed by onyx black lend an exotic feel to this distinctive afghan edged by lacy shells.

MOTIF A (make 28)
Rnd 1: With black, ch 8, sl st in first ch to form ring, ch 4, (dc, ch 1) 15 times in ring, join with sl st in 3rd ch of ch-4 (16 ch-1 sps).

Notes: For **beginning cluster (beg cl),** ch 3, (yo, insert hook in same sp, yo, draw lp through, yo, draw through 2 lps on hook) 2 times, yo, draw through all 3 lps on hook.

For **cluster (cl),** yo, insert hook in next ch sp, yo, draw lp through, yo, draw through 2 lps on hook, (yo, insert hook in same sp, yo, draw lp through, yo, draw through 2 lps on hook) 2 times, yo, draw through all 4 lps on hook.

For **beginning shell (beg shell),** ch 3, (3 dc, ch 2, 4 dc) in same sp.

For **shell,** (4 dc, ch 2, 4 dc) in next ch sp.

Rnd 2: Sl st in first ch sp, beg cl, ch 2, (cl in next ch sp, ch 2) around, join with sl st in first cl, fasten off.

Rnd 3: Join gold with sl st in any ch sp, beg shell, *[sc in next ch sp, (ch 3, sc in next ch sp) 2 times], shell in next ch sp; repeat from * 2 more times; repeat between [ ], join with sl st in top of ch-3, fasten off (12 sc, 8 ch-3 sps, 4 shells).

Rnd 4: Join green with sl st in ch sp of any shell, beg shell, 4 dc in each of next 2 ch sps, (shell in next ch sp, 4 dc in each of next 2 ch sps) around, join, fasten off (32 dc, 4 shells).

Rnd 5: Join black with sc in any st, sc in each st around with 3 sc in each corner ch sp, join with sl st in first sc, fasten off (76 sc).

MOTIF B (make 24)
Rnds 1-2: With blue, repeat same rnds of Motif A.

Rnd 3: With black, repeat same rnd of Motif A.

Rnds 4-5: Repeat same rnds of Motif A.

MOTIF C (make 18)
Rnds 1-2: Repeat same rnds of Motif A.

Rnd 3: With blue, repeat same rnd of Motif A.

Rnds 4-5: Repeat same rnds of Motif A.

Holding Motifs wrong sides together, matching sts, with black, sew together according to Assembly Diagram on page 42.

BORDER
Rnd 1: Join black with sc in center corner st before one short end, 2 sc in same st, (evenly space 131 sc across to next corner, 3 sc in next center corner st, evenly space 191 sc across long edge to next corner), 3 sc in next center corner st; repeat between ( ), join with sl st in first sc (133 sc on each short edge between center corner sts, 193 sc

Designed by
JoHanna Dzikowski

FINISHED SIZE
50" x 68½".

MATERIALS
Worsted-weight yarn —
33½ oz. black, 17 oz. green, 12½ oz. blue and 8½ oz. gold; tapestry needle; I crochet hook or size needed to obtain gauge.

GAUGE
Rnds 1-2 = 4" across.
Each Motif is 6¼" square.

SKILL LEVEL
Average

Continued on page 42

Burgundy Expressions

Bring luxurious comfort to your sitting room or parlor with a unique addition to your collection of sophisticated decorations.

Designed by
Daisy Watson

FINISHED SIZE
55" x 64".

MATERIALS
Worsted-weight yarn —
41 oz. burgundy and
13 oz. aran; I crochet
hook or size needed
to obtain gauge.

GAUGE
8 dc = 3"; 1 sc row
and 1 hdc row = 1".

SKILL LEVEL
Average

AFGHAN

Row 1: With burgundy, ch 166, sc in 2nd ch from hook, sc in each ch across, turn (165 sc).

Row 2: Ch 2, hdc in each st across, turn.

Row 3: Working in this row in **back lps** only, ch 3, dc in each st across, turn.

Note: For **cross stitch (cr st),** skip next 2 sts, tr in next st, ch 1; working over last tr made, tr in first skipped st.

Row 4: Working this row in **front lps** only, ch 3, dc in each of next 2 sts, (cr st, dc in each of next 3 sts) across, turn.

Row 5: Working this row in **back lps** only, ch 3, dc in each st and in each ch across, turn.

Row 6: Working this row in **front lps** only, ch 2, hdc in each st across, turn, fasten off.

Row 7: Working this row in **back lps** only, join aran with sl st in first st, ch 2, hdc in each st across, turn.

Note: For **shell,** dc in next st, (ch 1, dc) 3 times in same st.

Row 8: Ch 1, sc in each of first 2 sts, skip next 2 sts, shell in next st, skip next 2 sts, (sc in next st, skip next 2 sts, shell in next st, skip next 2 sts) across to last 2 sts, sc in each of last 2 sts, turn, fasten off (30 sc, 27 shells).

Row 9: Working this row in **back lps** only, join burgundy with sl st

in first st, ch 2, hdc in next st, (skip next st, hdc in next 5 chs and sts, skip next st, hdc in next st) across with hdc in last st, turn (165 hdc).

Rows 10-86: Repeat rows 2-9 consecutively, ending with row 6. At end of last row, **do not** fasten off.

BORDER

Rnd 1: Working around outer edge, ch 1, sc in each st across to last st, 3 sc in last st, evenly space 151 sc across ends of rows; working in starting ch on opposite side of row 1, 3 sc in first ch, sl st in each ch across with 3 sc in last ch, evenly space 151 sc across ends of rows, 2 sc in same st as first st, join with sl st in first sc, **turn** (153 sts on each short end between corner sts, 165 sts on each long edge between corner sts, 4 corner sts).

Rnd 2: Working this rnd in **back lps** only, ch 1, sc in first st, *[3 sc in next st, sc in each of next 2 sts, skip next 2 sts, shell in next st, skip next 2 sts], (sc in next st, skip next 2 sts, shell in next st, skip next 2 sts) across to 2 sts before next corner st, sc in each of next 2 sts; repeat from * 2 more times; repeat between [ ]; repeat between ( ) across to last st, sc in last st, join, **turn,** fasten off.

Rnd 3: Working in **remaining**

Continued on page 42

Blue Magic

*Let the enchanting radiance of this expressive beauty fill your room
with the gracious ambiance only fine needlework can create.*

Designed by
Shep Shepherd

FINISHED SIZE
48½" x 64".

MATERIALS
Bulky yarn — 32½ oz.
lt. blue, 12 oz. royal
blue and 8½ oz. white;
J crochet hook or
size needed to
obtain gauge.

GAUGE
Rnd 1 = 2" across.
Each Motif is
7¾" across.

SKILL LEVEL
Average

FIRST ROW
First Block
Rnd 1: With off-white, ch 6, sl st in first ch to form ring, ch 3, 15 dc in ring, join with sl st in top of ch-3, fasten off (16 dc).

Rnd 2: Join lt. blue with sl st in any st, ch 3, 2 dc in same st, ch 1, skip next st, (3 dc in next st, ch 1, skip next st) around, join (8 3-dc groups, 8 ch-1 sps).

Rnd 3: Ch 1, sc in each of first 3 sts, (*sc in next ch sp, ch 7, skip next 3 sts, sc in next ch sp*, sc in each of next 3 sts) 3 times; repeat between **, join with sl st in first sc (20 sc, 4 ch-7 sps).

Rnd 4: Sl st in next st, ch 1, sc in same st, *[(ch 1, tr) 4 times in next ch sp, ch 3, (tr, ch 1) 4 times in same sp as last tr, ch 1, skip next st], sc in next st; repeat from * 2 more times; repeat between [ ], join, fasten off.

Rnd 5: Join royal blue with sc in any corner ch-3 sp, ch 3, sc in same sp, *[ch 1, sc in next ch sp, ch 1, (sc, ch 3, sc) in next ch sp, ch 1, sc in next ch sp, ch 1, (sc, ch 5, sc) in next sc, ch 1, skip next ch-1 sp, sc in next ch-1 sp, ch 1, (sc, ch 3, sc) in next ch sp, ch 1, sc in next ch sp, ch 1], (sc, ch 3, sc, ch 3, sc) in next ch sp; repeat from * 2 more times; repeat between [ ], sc in same ch sp as first st, ch 3, join, fasten off.

Second Block
Rnds 1-4: Repeat same rnds of First Block.

Notes: For **joining ch-3 sp,** ch 1, sc in corresponding ch-3 sp on designated Motif, ch 1.

For **joining ch-5 sp,** ch 2, sc in corresponding ch-5 sp on designated Motif, ch 2.

Rnd 5: Join royal blue with sc in any corner ch-3 sp, ch 3, sc in same sp, *[ch 1, sc in next ch sp, ch 1, (sc, ch 3, sc) in next ch sp, ch 1, sc in next ch sp, ch 1, (sc, ch 5, sc) in next sc, ch 1, skip next ch-1 sp, sc in next ch-1 sp, ch 1, (sc, ch 3, sc) in next ch sp, ch 1, sc in next ch sp, ch 1], (sc, ch 3, sc, ch 3, sc) in next ch sp; repeat from *; repeat between [ ], (sc, ch 3, sc) in next ch sp; joining to side of last Block, work joining ch-3 sp in corresponding corner of last Block made, sc in same sp on this Block, ch 1, sc in next ch sp, ch 1, sc in next ch sp, work joining ch-3 sp, sc in same sp on this Block, ch 1, sc in next ch sp, ch 1, sc in next sc, work joining ch-5 sp, sc in same sc on this Block, ch 1, skip next ch-1 sp, sc in next ch-1 sp, ch 1, sc in next ch sp, work joining ch-3 sp, sc in same sp on this Block, ch 1, sc in next ch sp, ch 1, sc in same ch sp as first st, work joining ch-3 sp, join, fasten off.

Repeat Second Motif four more times for a total of six Motifs.

Continued on page 43

Petite Medallions

Like strands of pearls dipped in the morning dew, dainty crystals of light play across the filigreed surface of this mesmerizing cover.

FIRST STRIP
First Motif
Rnd 1: With white pompadour, ch 4, sl st in first ch to form ring, ch 1, 12 sc in ring, join with sl st in first sc (12 sc).

Rnd 2: Ch 3, dc in same st, ch 2, skip next st, (2 dc in next st, ch 2, skip next st) around, join with sl st in top of ch-3, fasten off (12 dc, 6 ch-2 sps).

Rnd 3: Join baby blue with sc in first st, ch 1, sc in next st; working around next ch sp, 3 dc in next skipped sc on rnd 1, (sc in next st, ch 1, sc in next st; working over next ch sp, 3 dc in next skipped st on rnd 1) around, join with sl st in first sc, fasten off (18 dc, 12 sc, 6 ch-1 sps).

Second Motif
Rnds 1-2: Repeat same rnds of First Motif.

Rnd 3: Join baby blue with sc in first st, ch 1, sc in next st; working around next ch sp, 3 dc in next skipped sc on rnd 1, (sc in next st, ch 1, sc in next st; working over next ch sp, 3 dc in next skipped st on rnd 1) 4 times, sc in next st, ch 1, sl st in 3rd ch-1 sp on last Motif made, ch 1, sc in next st on this Motif; working over next ch sp, 3 dc in next skipped st on rnd 1, join with sl st in first sc, fasten off.

Repeat Second Motif eighteen more times for a total of twenty Motifs.

Border
Notes: For **reverse shell (rev shell),** (yo, insert hook in next st, yo, draw lp through, yo, draw through 2 lps on hook) 4 times, skip next joining, (yo, insert hook in next st, yo, draw lp through, yo, draw through 2 lps on hook) 4 times, yo, draw through all 9 lps on hook.

For **sc decrease (sc dec),** insert hook in next dc, yo, draw lp through, skip next rev shell, insert hook in next dc, yo, draw lp through, yo, draw through all 3 lps on hook.

Rnd 1: Working this rnd in **back lps** only, join white with sl st in first sc of 2 sc-group after joining on First Motif, ch 5, [dc in next sc, ch 2, (skip next dc, dc in next dc, ch 2, skip next dc, dc in next sc, ch 2, dc in next sc, ch 2) 4 times, rev shell; *ch 1, (dc in next st or ch, ch 1) 9 times, rev shell; repeat from * 17 more times, ch 2], dc in next sc, ch 2; repeat between [ ], join with sl st in 3rd ch of ch-5, fasten off.

Rnd 2: Join baby blue with sc in 3rd ch sp, sc in same sp, [(sc in next st; for **picot,** ch 3, sl st in top of last sc made; 2 sc in next ch sp) 10 times, sc dec, *sc in next ch sp, (sc in next st, picot, sc in next ch sp) 7 times, sc dec; repeat from * 17 more times, 2 sc in next ch sp, sc in next st, picot, 2 sc in next ch sp, sc in next st, picot], 2 sc in next ch sp;

Continued on page 43

Designed by Sandra Smith

FINISHED SIZE
45" x 68".

MATERIALS
Sport yarn — 25 oz. baby blue and 12 oz. white; pompadour sport yarn — 11 oz. white; G crochet hook or size needed to obtain gauge.

GAUGE
Rnds 1-3 of Motif = 2½" across.

SKILL LEVEL
Average

Stars in the Mist

An ethereal halo seems to envelope this downy soft statement of refined good taste that uses an heirloom-style motif design.

Designed by
Maggie Weldon
*for Monsanto's
Designs for America
Program*

FINISHED SIZE
50" x 70".

MATERIALS
Fuzzy chunky yarn —
50 oz. fisherman;
tapestry needle;
J crochet hook or
size needed to
obtain gauge.

GAUGE
3 sts = 1"; 2 dc rows =
1¼". Each Motif
is 8" across.

SKILL LEVEL
Average

MOTIF (make 53)

Rnd 1: Ch 2, 6 sc in 2nd ch from hook, join with sl st in first sc (6 sc).

Note: For **curlicue,** ch 10, 4 sc in 2nd ch from hook, 4 sc in each ch across.

Rnd 2: Curlicue, sl st in first st, sl st in next st, (curlicue, sl st in same st, sl st in next st) 4 times, curlicue, sl st in same st, sl st in same st as first curlicue.

Note: For **double treble crochet (dtr),** yo 3 times, insert hook in next st, yo, draw lp through, (yo, draw through 2 lps on hook) 4 times.

Rnd 3: Ch 9, sc in tip of next curlicue, ch 4, (dtr in sl st between last worked curlicue and next curlicue, ch 4, sc in top of next curlicue, ch 4) around, join with sl st in 5th ch of ch-9.

Rnd 4: Ch 3, *[3 dc in next ch sp, (dc, ch 2, dc) in next sc, 3 dc in next ch sp], dc in next dtr; repeat from * 4 more times; repeat between [ ], join with sl st in top of ch-3.

Rnd 5: Sl st in next st, ch 4, skip next st, dc in next st, ch 1, skip next st, *(dc, ch 2, dc) in next ch-2 sp, ch 1, skip next st, (dc in next st, ch 1, skip next st) 4 times; repeat from * 4 more times, (dc, ch 2, dc) in next ch-2 sp, ch 1, skip next st, (dc in next st, ch 1, skip next st) 2 times, join with sl st in 3rd ch of ch-4.

Rnd 6: Ch 1, sc in each st and in each ch-1 sp around with 3 sc in each ch-2 sp, join with sl st in first sc, fasten off (84 sc).

Holding Motifs wrong sides together, matching sts, sew together through **back lps** according to Assembly Diagram.

BORDER

Notes: For **picot,** ch 4, sl st in 3rd ch from hook, ch 1.

Border is worked in sc on last rnd and ch-2 sps on rnd before last.

Working over 3 sc on last rnd into ch-2 sp on rnd before last, join with sl st in ch sp indicated on diagram, (ch 3, picot, dc) in same sp, (picot, skip next st, dc in next st) around with (picot, dc, picot, dc) in each ch-2 sp on rnd before last and (picot, dc ch-2 sps on each side of seams tog) at each seam, join with sl st in top of ch-3, fasten off.

ASSEMBLY DIAGRAM

← Join here
for Border

Laura's Roses

Continued from page 30

join, fasten off (20 sc on each side between corner ch sps).

With mauve, sew Blocks together in seven rows of nine Blocks each.

BORDER

Rnd 1: Join mauve with sc in any corner ch sp, ch 2, sc in same sp, sc in each st and in each ch sp on each side of seams around with (sc, ch 2, sc) in each corner ch sp, join with sl st in first sc, fasten off (154 sc on each short end, 198 sc on each long edge, 4 ch-2 sps).

Rnd 2: Join black with sc in corner ch sp

before one short end, ch 2, sc in same sp, *ch 2, skip next st, (sc next 2 sts tog, ch 2, skip next st) across to next corner ch sp, (sc, ch 2, sc) in next corner ch sp, ch 2, skip next 2 sts, sc next 2 sts tog, (ch 2, skip next st, sc next 2 sts tog) across to 2 sts before next corner ch sp, ch 2, skip next 2 sts*, (sc, ch 2, sc) in next corner ch sp; repeat between **, join, fasten off.

Rnd 3: Join dk. rose with sl st in any sc, ch 1, bs in next ch sp, (sl st in next sc, ch 1, bs in next ch sp) around, join with sl st in first sl st, fasten off.

Rnd 4: Working over sl sts on last rnd into sc on rnd 2, join black with sl st in any sc, ch 3, 2 dc in same sc, (sl st, ch 3, 2 dc) in each sc around, join with sl st in first sl st, fasten off.

Cloisonñe

Continued from page 33

on each long edge between center corner sts).

Rnd 2: Ch 1, sc in first st, *ch 4, skip next st, sc in next st, (ch 4, skip next 2 sts, sc in next st) across to next corner st; repeat from * 2 more times, ch 4, skip next st, (sc in next st, ch 4, skip next 2 sts) across, join (44 ch sps between corner ch sps on each short edge, 64 ch sps between corner ch sps on each long edge, 4 corner ch sps).

Rnd 3: Sl st in first ch sp, ch 4, (3 tr, ch 3, 4 tr) in same sp, *[ch 3, skip next ch sp, (sc in next ch sp, ch 3) 2 times, skip next ch sp], (4 tr, ch 3, 4 tr) in next ch sp; repeat from * around to last 4 ch sps; repeat between [ ],

join with sl st in top of ch-4.

Rnd 4: Sl st in each of next 3 sts, sl st in next ch sp, ch 1, sc in same sp, (ch 3, sc in same sp) 3 times, *[ch 5, 3 sc in next ch sp, 4 sc in next ch sp, 3 sc in next ch sp, ch 5], sc in next ch sp, (ch 3, sc in same sp) 3 times; repeat from * around to last 3 ch sps; repeat between [ ], join with sl st in first sc, fasten off.

ASSEMBLY DIAGRAM

A	A	B	C	B	A	A
A	B	C	A	C	B	A
B	C	A	B	A	C	B
C	A	B	C	B	A	C
A	B	A	B	A	B	A
A	B	C	B	C	B	A
C	A	B	C	B	A	C
B	C	A	B	A	C	B
A	B	C	A	C	B	A
A	A	B	C	B	A	A

A = Motif A
B = Motif B
C = Motif C

Burgundy Expressions

Continued from page 34

lps on rnd 1, join aran with sc in any corner st, *[sc in next st, (ch 2, skip next st, sc in next st) 2 times, (ch 2, skip next 2 sts, sc in next st) across to 4 sts before next corner st, (ch 2, skip next st, sc in next st) 2 times],

sc in next corner st; repeat from * 2 more times; repeat between [ ], join.

Rnd 4: Ch 3, 4 dc in same st, [◊sc in each of next 2 sc, *dc in next sc, (ch 1, dc) 4 times in same sc, sc in next sc; repeat from * across to last sc before next corner sc, sc in next sc◊, 5 dc in next sc]; repeat between [ ] 2 more times; repeat between ◊◊, join with sl st in top of ch-3, fasten off.

Petite Medallions

Continued from page 39

repeat between [ ], join with sl st in first sc, fasten off.

SECOND STRIP
Motifs

Work same as Motifs of First Strip.

Border

Rnd 1: Repeat same rnd of Border on First Strip.

Rnd 2: Join baby blue with sc in 3rd ch sp, sc in same sp, (sc in next st, picot, 2 sc in next ch

sp) 10 times, sc dec, *sc in next ch sp, (sc in next st, picot, sc in next ch sp) 7 times, sc dec; repeat from * 17 more times, 2 sc in next ch sp, (sc in next st, picot, 2 sc in next ch sp) 10 times, sc in next st; for **joining picot,** ch 1, sl st in corresponding picot on last Strip made, ch 1, sl st in top of last sc; 2 sc in next ch sp, sc in next st, joining picot, 2 sc in next ch sp, sc dec, [sc in next ch sp, (sc in next st, picot, sc in next ch sp) 2 times, (sc in next st, joining picot, sc in next ch sp) 3 times, (sc in next st, picot, sc in next ch sp) 2 times, sc dec]; repeat between [ ] 17 more times, (2 sc in next ch sp, sc in next st, joining picot) 2 times, join with sl st in first sc, fasten off.

Repeat Second Strip seven more times for a total of nine Strips.

Blue Magic

Continued from page 36

SECOND ROW
First Block

Joining to bottom of First Block on last row, work same as First Row Second Block.

Second Block

Rnds 1-4: Repeat same rnds of First Block on First Row.

Rnd 5: Join royal blue with sc in any corner ch-3 sp, ch 3, sc in same sp, *ch 1, sc in next ch sp, ch 1, (sc, ch 3, sc) in next ch sp, ch 1, sc in next ch sp, ch 1, (sc, ch 5, sc) in next sc, ch 1, skip next ch-1 sp, sc in next ch-1 sp, ch 1, (sc, ch 3, sc) in next ch sp, ch 1, sc in next ch sp, ch 1*, (sc, ch 3, sc, ch 3, sc) in next ch sp; repeat between **, (sc, ch 3, sc) in next ch sp; joining to bottom of next Block on row above, work joining ch-3 sp in corresponding corner ch sp, [sc in same sp on this Block, ch 1, sc in next ch sp, ch 1, sc in next ch sp, work joining ch-3 sp, sc in same sp on this Block, ch 1, sc in next ch sp, ch 1, sc in next sc, work joining ch-5 sp, sc in same sc on this Block, ch 1, skip next ch-1 sp, sc in next ch-1 sp, ch 1, sc in next ch sp, work joining ch-3 sp, sc in same sp on this Block, ch 1, sc in next ch sp, ch 1, sc in next

ch sp, work joining ch-3 sp], sc in same sp on this Block; joining to side of last Block on this row, work joining ch-3 sp; repeat between [ ], join, fasten off.

Repeat Second Motif four more times for a total of six Motifs.

Repeat Second Row six more times for a total of eight Rows.

BORDER

Rnd 1: Join off-white with sc in 2nd ch-3 sp on any corner, ch 3, sc in same sp, ◊[*ch 1, (sc in next ch sp, ch 1) 2 times, (sc, ch 3, sc) in next ch sp*; repeat between ** 3 more times, ch 1, sc in joining sc, ch 1, skip next ch sp, (sc, ch 3, sc) in next ch sp]; repeat between [ ] across to last Motif on this side; repeat between ** 4 times, (sc, ch 3, sc) in next ch sp◊; repeat between ◊◊ 2 times; repeat between [ ] across to last Motif on this side; repeat between ** 4 times, join with sl st in first sc.

Rnd 2: Sl st in next ch sp, ch 1, (sc, ch 3, sc) in same sp, ◊[*ch 1, (sc in next ch sp, ch 1) 3 times, (sc, ch 3, sc) in next ch sp*; repeat between ** 3 more times, ch 1, (sc in next ch sp, ch 1) 2 times, (sc, ch 3, sc) in next ch sp]; repeat between [ ] across to last Motif on this side; repeat between ** 4 times, (sc, ch 3, sc) in next ch sp◊; repeat between ◊◊ 2 times; repeat between [ ] across to last Motif on this side; repeat between ** 4 times, join, fasten off.

Sun Room
Splendor

Lavender Fascination

As sunshine reflects a rainbow of colors in the morning dew, so this alluring geometric pattern shines with fresh-as-spring appeal.

BLOCK (make 24)

Note: For **shell,** (3 dc, ch 2, 3 dc) in next ch or st.

Rnd 1: Starting at center, with lavender, ch 42, sc in 2nd ch from hook, *skip next 3 chs, shell in next ch, skip next 3 chs, (sc in next ch, skip next 3 chs, shell in next ch, skip next 3 chs) across to last ch*, (sc, ch 2, sc) in last ch; working on opposite side of starting ch, repeat between **, sc in last ch, ch 2, join with sl st in first sc, fasten off (12 sc, 10 shells, 2 ch-2 sps).

Row 2: Working in rows, join variegated with sc in 2nd dc of first shell, sc in next st, (sc, ch 2, sc) in next ch sp, *sc in each of next 3 sts, skip next st, sc in each of next 3 sts, (sc, ch 2, sc) in next ch sp; repeat from * 3 more times, sc in each of next 2 sts leaving remaining sts unworked, turn (38 sc, 5 ch sps).

Row 3: Ch 1, skip first st, sc next 2 sts tog, (sc, ch 2, sc) in next ch sp, *sc in each of next 3 sts, sc next 2 sts tog, sc in each of next 3 sts, (sc, ch 2, sc) in next ch sp; repeat from * across to last 3 sts, sc next 2 sts tog leaving last st unworked, turn, fasten off (40 sc, 5 ch sps).

Row 4: Join green with sc in first ch sp, (skip next 4 sts, shell in next st, skip next 4 sts, sc in next ch sp) across leaving last 2 sts unworked, **do not** turn, fasten off (5 sc, 4 shells).

Row 5: Skip first 2 sts, join variegated with sc in next st, sc in next st, (sc, ch 2, sc) in next ch sp, *sc in each of next 3 sts, skip next st, sc in each of next 3 sts, (sc, ch 2, sc) in next ch sp; repeat from * across to last 4 sts, sc in each of next 2 sts leaving remaining sts unworked, turn (30 sc, 4 ch sps).

Row 6: Repeat row 3 (31 sc, 4 ch sps).

Row 7: With lavender, repeat row 4 (4 sc, 3 shells).

Rows 8-9: Repeat rows 5 and 3, ending with 22 sc and 3 ch sps in last row.

Row 10: Repeat row 4 (3 sc, 2 shells).

Row 11: Skip first 2 sts, join variegated with sc in next st, sc in next st, (sc, ch 2, sc) in next ch sp, sc in each of next 3 sts, skip next st, sc in each of next 3 sts, (sc, ch 2, sc) in next ch sp, sc in each of next 2 sts leaving last 2 sts unworked, turn (14 sc, 2 ch sps).

Row 12: Ch 1, skip first st, sc next 2 sts tog, (sc, ch 2, sc) in next ch sp, sc in each of next 3 sts, sc next 2 sts tog, sc in each of next 3 sts, (sc, ch 2, sc) in next ch sp, sc next 2 sts tog leaving last st unworked, turn, fasten off (13 sc, 2 ch sps).

Row 13: Join lavender with sc in first ch sp, skip next 4 sts, shell in next st, skip next 4 sts, sc in next

Designed by
Katherine Eng

FINISHED SIZE
45" x 63½".

MATERIALS
Worsted-weight yarn —
33 oz. lavender,
22 oz. variegated and
10 oz. green; tapestry
needle; H crochet
hook or size needed
to obtain gauge.

GAUGE
7 sts = 2"; 1 shell
row and 2 sc rows =
1½". Each Block is
9¼" square.

SKILL LEVEL
Average

Continued on page 54

Wish Upon a Star

Myriad jeweltone shades create a vibrant background for this star-studded cover, reminiscent of a patchwork comforter.

Designed by
Sandra Miller Maxfield

FINISHED SIZE
46½" x 60".

MATERIALS
Worsted-weight yarn —
55 oz. scrap yarn in
assorted colors and
8 oz. white; tapestry
needle; H crochet
hook or size needed
to obtain gauge.

GAUGE
Rnd 1 of Motif = 1⅝"
across. Each Motif
is 4½" square.

SKILL LEVEL
Average

MOTIF (make 130)

Rnd 1: With scrap yarn, ch 3, sl st in first ch to form ring, ch 3, 11 dc in ring, join with sl st in top of ch-3, fasten off (12 dc).

Rnd 2: Join white with sl st in any st, ch 5, sl st in next st, ch 10, skip next st, (sl st in next st, ch 5, sl st in next st, ch 10, skip next st) around, join with sl st in first sl st, fasten off (4 ch-5 lps, 4 ch-10 lps).

Rnd 3: Working behind ch-10 lps, join scrap yarn with sl st in any skipped st on rnd 1, ch 3, (*dc in same st on rnd 1 as next sl st, ch 2, sc in next ch-5 lp, ch 2, dc in same st on rnd 1 as next sl st*, dc in next skipped st on rnd 1) 3 times; repeat between **, join with sl st in top of ch-3 (12 dc, 8 ch-2 sps, 4 sc).

Rnd 4: Sl st in next st, sl st in next ch sp, ch 3, 2 dc in same sp, (*ch 2, 3 dc in next ch sp, dc in next st, ch 8, skip next st*, dc in next st, 3 dc in next ch sp) 3 times; repeat between **, dc in same st as first sl st, join (32 dc, 4 ch-2 sps, 4 ch-8 lps).

Notes: For **front post stitch** (*fp, see fig. 9, page 159*), yo, insert hook from front to back around post of next st, yo, draw

lp through, (yo, draw through 2 lps on hook) 2 times.

To **twist ch lps,** fold next ch-10 lp on rnd 2 left to right forming a loop; with crochet hook, draw next ch-8 lp on rnd 4 through loop.

Rnd 5: Ch 3, fp around each of next 2 sts, *[(3 dc, ch 2, 3 dc) in next ch sp, fp around next 4 sts, twist ch lps, sc in same ch-8 lp], fp around next 4 sts; repeat from * 2 more times; repeat between [ ], fp around last st, join, fasten off.

Holding Motifs wrong sides together, matching sts, sew together through **back lps** only in ten rows of thirteen Motifs each.

EDGING

Rnd 1: Working around entire outer edge, join white with sc in any corner ch sp, (sc, ch 2, 2 sc) in same sp, sc in each st around with (sc next 2 ch sps tog) at each seam and (2 sc, ch 2, 2 sc) in each corner ch sp, join with sl st in first sc.

Rnd 2: Ch 2, hdc in each st around with (2 hdc, ch 2, 2 hdc) in each corner ch sp, join with sl st in top of ch-2, fasten off.

Spring Lattice

Garden hues of iris purple, leaf green and sunny yellow twined on a lacy white trellis give tender innocence to this feminine design.

Designed by
Shep Shepherd

FINISHED SIZE
43" x 67".

MATERIALS
Worsted-weight yarn —
24 oz. white, 7 oz.
yellow, 4 oz. purple
and 2½ oz. green;
H crochet hook or
size needed to
obtain gauge.

GAUGE
Row 1 = 2¼" across;
11 hdc rows = 6".

SKILL LEVEL
Average

PANEL NO. 1
Strip (make 2)

Notes: Ch-6 at end of row 1 counts as first hdc and ch-2 sp.

Ch-4 at beginning of each remaining row counts as first hdc and ch-2 sp.

For **shell,** (4 hdc, ch 4, 4 hdc) in next ch sp.

Row 1: With white, ch 13, hdc in 7th ch from hook, (ch 2, skip next 2 chs, hdc in next ch) 2 times, turn (4 hdc, 3 ch-2 sps).

Row 2: Ch 4, hdc in next hdc, ch 2, skip next hdc, shell in last ch sp, turn (2 hdc, 2 ch-2 sps, 1 shell).

Row 3: Ch 4, shell in next ch sp, ch 2, skip next 3 hdc, hdc in next hdc, ch 2, hdc in next hdc, ch 2, hdc in 2nd ch of last ch-4, turn (4 hdc, 4 ch-2 sps, 1 shell).

Row 4: Ch 4, hdc in next hdc, (ch 2, hdc in next hdc) 2 times leaving remaining sts unworked, turn (4 hdc, 3 ch-2 sps).

Row 5: Ch 4, hdc in next hdc, ch 2, hdc in next hdc, ch 2, hdc in 2nd ch of last ch-4, turn.

Row 6: Ch 4, hdc in next hdc, ch 2, skip next hdc, shell in last ch sp, ch 2, sl st in ch sp of shell 2 rows before last, turn.

Row 7: Ch 2, shell in ch sp of next shell, ch 2, skip next 3 hdc, hdc in next hdc, ch 2, hdc in next hdc, ch 2, hdc in 2nd ch of last ch-4, turn.

Rows 8-119: Repeat rows 4-7 consecutively. At end of last row, fasten off.

For **trim,** join purple with sl st in center ch sp on opposite side of row 1; working vertically across center of Strip, (ch 3, sl st in ch sp on next row) across, fasten off.

To **join,** hold Strips side by side, matching ends of rows without shells; working in sps at ends of rows, join green with sl st in first row on first Strip, ch 3, sl st in end of first row on 2nd Strip, (ch 3, skip next row on first Strip, sl st in next row, ch 3, skip next row on 2nd Strip, sl st in next row) across, fasten off.

Edging

For **first side,** working across one long edge of panel, join yellow with sc in first ch sp, ch 5, sc in next ch sp, (ch 3, sc in next ch sp, ch 5, sc in next ch sp) across, fasten off.

For **2nd side,** repeat on opposite long edge.

PANELS NO. 2-5
Strip (make 2)

Work and join same as Panel No. 1 Strip.

Edging

For **first side,** work same as

Continued on page 54

Sunflowers

Drift away in remembrances of childhood ventures under a cloudless summer sky with this country look afghan, created patchwork-style.

BLOCK (make 12)
Center
Row 1: With brown, ch 35, sc in 2nd ch from hook, sc in each ch across, turn (34 sc).

Rows 2-19: Ch 1, sc in each st across, turn. At end of last row, fasten off.

Row 20: Skip first 8 sts, join brown with sc in next st, sc in next 17 sts leaving remaining sts unworked, turn (18).

Rows 21-28: Ch 1, sc in each st across, turn. At end of last row, fasten off.

Row 29: Working in starting ch on opposite side of row 1, with wrong side of row 1 facing you, skip first 8 chs, join brown with sc in next ch, sc in next 17 chs leaving remaining chs unworked, turn (18).

Rows 30-37: Ch 1, sc in each st across, turn. At end of last row, fasten off.

Piece No. 1 (make 4)
Row 1: With brown, ch 2, sc in 2nd ch from hook, turn (1 sc).

Row 2: Ch 1, 3 sc in first st, turn (3).

Rows 3-7: Ch 1, 2 sc in first st, sc in each st across with 2 sc in last st, turn, ending with 13 sc in last row. At end of last row, fasten off.

Row 8: Join yellow with sl st in first st, ch 1, sc same st and next st tog, sc in each st across to last 2 sts, sc last 2 sts tog, turn (11).

Rows 9-12: Ch 1, sc first 2 sts tog, sc in each st across to last 2 sts, sc last 2 sts tog, turn, ending with 3 sc in last row.

Row 13: Ch 1, sc in first st, sc last 2 sts tog, turn (2).

Row 14: Ch 1, sc first 2 sts tog, fasten off (1).

Piece No. 2 (make 16)
Rows 1-7: With yellow, repeat same rows of Piece No. 1.

Rows 8-14: With blue, repeat same rows of Piece No. 1.

Piece No. 3 (make 4)
Row 1: With blue, ch 9, sc in 2nd ch from hook, sc in each ch across, turn (8 sc).

Rows 2-8: Ch 1, sc in each st across, turn. At end of last row, fasten off.

ASSEMBLY
To **form Block,** using matching colors, sew all Pieces together according to Block Assembly Diagram.

For **Block edging,** working around outer edge of Block, join blue with sc in any corner st, 2 sc in same st, sc in each st and in end of each row around with 3 sc in each corner, join with sl st in first sc, fasten off.

Continued on page 54

Designed by Barbara Roy

FINISHED SIZE
45" x 58".

MATERIALS
Worsted-weight yarn — 33 oz. blue, 25 oz. brown and 20 oz. yellow; tapestry needle; G crochet hook or size needed to obtain gauge.

GAUGE
4 sc = 1";
4 sc rows = 1".

SKILL LEVEL
Average

BLOCK ASSEMBLY DIAGRAM

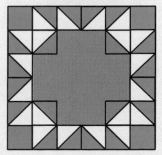

Sunflowers

Continued from page 53

With blue, sew Blocks together in three rows of four Blocks each.

BORDER

Rnd 1: Working around entire outer edge, join blue with sc in any corner st, 2 sc in same st, sc in each st around with 3 sc in each corner, join with sl st in first sc.

Rnds 2-6: Ch 1, sc in each st around, join.

Rnd 7: Ch 1; working from left to right, **reverse sc** *(see fig. 10, page 159)* in each st around, join, fasten off.

Spring Lattice

Continued from page 50

Panel No. 1 Edging.

For **2nd side,** working across opposite long edge, join yellow with sc in first ch sp; to **join Panels,** holding Panel you are working against last Panel made, ch 2, sc in first ch-5 sp of Edging on previous Panel, ch 2, sc in next ch sp on Panel you are working, *ch 1, sc in next ch-3 sp on other Panel, ch 1, sc in next ch sp on this Panel, ch 2, sc in next ch-5 sp on other Panel, ch 2, sc in next ch sp on this Panel; repeat from * across, fasten off.

BORDER

Rnd 1: Working around entire outer edge of Panels, with right side facing you, join yellow with sc in ch sp of corner shell before either short end, ch 5, sc in same sp, [ch 5, sc in next ch sp, ch 3, sc in next ch sp, (ch 5, skip next ch sp, sc in next Strip joining or in next ch sp, ch 3, sc in next ch sp) 2 times, ch 5, skip next Panel joining, *sc in next ch sp, ch 3, sc in next ch sp, ch 5, skip next ch sp, sc in next ch sp, ch 3, sc in next Strip joining, ch 5, skip next ch sp, sc in next ch sp, ch 3, sc in next ch sp, ch 5, skip next ch sp, sc in next Panel joining; repeat from * 2 more times, sc in next ch sp, ch 3, sc in next ch sp, ch 5, skip next ch sp, sc in next ch sp, ch 3, sc in next Strip joining, ch 5, skip next ch sp, sc in next ch sp, ch 3, sc in next ch sp, ch 5, (sc, ch 5, sc) in next corner ch sp; working across long edge, ch 5, (sc in next ch sp, ch 3, sc in next ch sp, ch 5) across to corner shell], (sc, ch 5, sc) in ch sp of corner shell; repeat between [ ], join with sl st in first sc.

Rnd 2: Sl st in first ch sp, ch 1, (3 sc, ch 3, 3 sc) in same sp, (3 sc, ch 3, 3 sc) in each ch-5 sp and (sc, ch 3, sc) in each ch-3 sp around, join, fasten off.

Lavender Fascination

Continued from page 47

ch sp leaving last 2 sts unworked, **do not** turn, fasten off (2 sc, 1 shell).

Row 14: Working in unworked sts on opposite side of rnd 1, join variegated with sc in 2nd dc of next unworked shell, sc in next st, (sc, ch 2, sc) in next ch sp, *sc in each of next 3 sts, skip next st, sc in each of next 3 sts, (sc, ch 2, sc) in next ch sp; repeat from * 3 more times, sc in each of next 2 sts leaving remaining sts unworked, turn (38 sc, 5 ch sps).

Rows 15-25: Repeat rows 3-13. At end of last row, **do not** fasten off.

Rnd 26: Working in sts and in ends of rows, ch 1, evenly space 20 sc across to next corner ch-2 sp, (sc, ch 2, sc) in corner ch sp, *evenly space 24 sc across to next corner ch sp, (sc, ch 2, sc) in corner ch sp; repeat from * 2 more times, sc in last 4 sts, **do not** turn, join with sl st in first sc (26 sc across each edge between corner ch sps).

Rnd 27: Ch 1, sc in each st around with (sc, ch 3, sc) in each corner ch sp, join, fasten off (28 sc on each edge between corner ch sps).

Matching sts and chs, sew Blocks together through **back lps** only according to Assembly Diagram.

BORDER

Rnd 1: Working around entire outer edge, with wrong side of work facing you, join lavender with sc in any corner ch sp, ch 3, sc in same sp, sc in each st, sc in each ch sp on each side of seams and hdc in each seam around with (sc, ch 3, sc) in each corner ch sp, join with sl st in first sc, **turn** (123 sc on each short edge between corner ch sps, 185 sc on each long edge between corner ch sps).

Rnd 2: Ch 1, sc in each st around with (sc, ch 3, sc) in each corner ch sp, **do not** turn, join.

Rnd 3: Ch 1, sc in first st, *ch 1, skip next st, (sc in next st, ch 1, skip next st) across to next corner ch sp, (sc, ch 3, sc) in next corner ch sp; repeat from * 3 more times, ch 1, skip last st, join, fasten off.

Rnd 4: Join variegated with sc in any corner ch sp, ch 3, sc in same sp, sc in each st and in each ch-1 sp around with (sc, ch 3, sc) in each corner ch sp, join, **turn.**

Rnd 5: Repeat rnd 2, **turn,** fasten off.

Rnd 6: Join green with sl st in any corner ch sp, ch 3, (dc, ch 2, 2 dc) in same sp, dc in each st around with (2 dc, ch 2, 2 dc) in each corner ch sp, join with sl st in top of ch-3, **turn.**

Rnd 7: Repeat rnd 3, **turn.**

Rnds 8-9: Repeat rnds 4 and 5.

Notes: For **beginning corner shell (beg corner shell),** ch 3, (2 dc, ch 3, 3 dc) in same sp.

For **corner shell,** (3 dc, ch 3, 3 dc) in next corner ch sp.

Rnd 10: Join lavender with sl st in corner ch sp before one short end, beg corner shell, *skip next st, sc in next st, (skip next 2 sts, shell in next st, skip next 2 sts, sc in next st) across to one st before next corner ch sp, skip next st, corner shell, skip next 2 sts, sc

in next st, skip next 2 sts, (shell in next st, skip next 2 sts, sc in next 2 sts, skip next 2 sts) across to next corner ch sp*, corner shell; repeat between **, join with sl st in top of ch-3.

Rnd 11: Sl st in each of next 2 sts, sl st in next ch sp, beg corner shell, *[skip next st, sc in next st, skip next st, shell in next sc, (sc in ch sp of next shell, shell in next sc) across to next corner shell, skip next st, sc in next st, skip next st], corner shell; repeat from * 2 more times; repeat between [ ], join.

Rnd 12: Sl st in each of next 2 sts, sl st in next ch sp, ch 1, sc in same sp, [◊(ch 3, sc) 3 times in same sp, ch 3, sc in next sc, ch 3, *(sc, ch 3, sc) in ch sp of next shell, ch 3, sc in next sc, ch 3; repeat from * across to next corner ch sp◊, sc in next ch sp]; repeat between [ ] 2 times; repeat between ◊◊, join with sl st in first sc, fasten off.

ASSEMBLY DIAGRAM

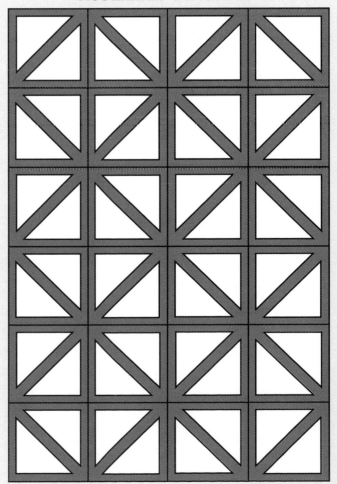

Flower Fantasy

Fairies and fireflies seem just around the corner when you gaze at this fanciful bouquet of blooms and buds.

Designed by
Shep Shepherd

FINISHED SIZE
53" x 62".

MATERIALS
Worsted-weight yarn —
17 oz. lt. pink, 14 oz.
dk. pink and 6 oz.
green; J crochet hook
or size needed to
obtain gauge.

GAUGE
3 sts = 1"; Rnds 1-2
of Large Motif = 2½"
across. Finished
Large Motif is
8¾" across.

SKILL LEVEL
Advanced

FIRST ROW
First Large Motif
Rnd 1: With dk. pink, ch 8, sl st in first ch to form ring, ch 2, 11 hdc in ring, join with sl st in top of ch-2, fasten off (12 hdc).

Rnd 2: Working this rnd in **back lps** only, join lt. pink with sl st in any st, ch 2, hdc in same st, 2 hdc in each st around, join, fasten off (24).

Rnd 3: Working this rnd in **back lps** only, join green with sl st in any st, ch 5, skip next st, (sl st in next st, ch 5, skip next st) around, join with sl st in first sl st, fasten off (12 ch lps).

Rnd 4: For **petals,** join lt. pink with sc in any ch lp, ch 10, dc in 6th ch from hook, dc in next 4 chs, (sc in next ch lp, ch 10, dc in 6th ch from hook, dc in next 4 chs) around, join with sl st in first sc, fasten off (12 petals).

Note: For **shell,** (sc, ch 2, 2 dc, ch 2, 2 dc, ch 2, sc) in ch sp at top of next petal.

Rnd 5: Working in opposite side of ch-10 on first petal, skip first 2 chs after joining sc of rnd 4, join dk. pink with sc in next ch, *[sc in each of next 2 chs; working in ch-5 lps at ends of petals, shell in each of next 3 petals, sc in each of next 3 dc on same petal as last shell made], skip first 2 chs on opposite side of ch-10 on next petal, sc in next ch; repeat from * 2

more times; repeat between [ ], join with sl st in first sc, fasten off.

Second Large Motif
Rnds 1-4: Repeat same rnds of First Large Motif.

Note: For **joining shell,** (sc, ch 2, 2 dc) in ch-5 lp at end of next petal, ch 1, sl st in center ch sp of shell on corresponding petal, ch 1, (2 dc, ch 2, sc) in same ch-5 lp on this Motif.

Rnd 5: Working in opposite side of ch-10 on first petal, skip first 2 chs after joining sc of rnd 4, join dk. pink with sc in next ch, *sc in each of next 2 chs; working in ch-5 lps at ends of petals, shell in each of next 3 petals, sc in each of next 3 dc on same petal as last shell made, skip first 2 chs on opposite side of ch-10 on next petal, sc in next ch; repeat from * 2 more times, sc in each of next 2 chs; joining to side of last Large Motif made (see Motif Diagram on page 61), work joining shell in each of next 3 petals, sc in each of next 3 dc on same petal as last joining shell made, join with sl st in first sc, fasten off.

Repeat Second Large Motif four more times for a total of six Motifs in First Row.

SECOND ROW
First Large Motif
Joining to bottom of First Large

Continued on page 61

American Beauty

Long revered as the symbol of undying devotion, this captivating portrait of the flower of love captures Mother Nature at her finest.

AFGHAN

Row 1: With raspberry, ch 121, sc in 2nd ch from hook, sc in each ch across, turn (120 sc).

Rows 2-6: Ch 1, sc in each st across, turn.

Notes: Wind raspberry into 3 large balls and one small ball. Wind green into 3 balls.

When changing colors *(see fig. 11, page 159),* always drop yarn to wrong side of work. Use a separate skein or ball of yarn for each color section. When working body of rose, carry colored yarn across from one section to another under white yarn as indicated on graph. Do not carry colors across background. Fasten off colors at end of each color section.

Work odd-numbered graph rows from right to left and even-numbered rows from left to right.

Row 7: For row 7 of graph, ch 1, sc in first 5 sts changing to white in last st made; carrying dropped raspberry across under white, sc in next 110 sts changing to raspberry in last st made, drop white; with raspberry only, sc in last 5 sts, turn.

Rows 8-155: Ch 1, sc in each st across changing colors according to graph, turn.

Rows 156-161: Ch 1, sc in each st across, turn. At end of last row, fasten off.

Graph on page 60

Designed by
Rhonda Simpson

FINISHED SIZE
51½" x 60½".

MATERIALS
Worsted-weight yarn —
24 oz. white, 15 oz.
raspberry and 8 oz.
green; J crochet hook
or size needed to
obtain gauge.

GAUGE
7 sc = 3";
8 sc rows = 3".

SKILL LEVEL
Average

American Beauty *Instructions on page 59*

COLOR CHANGE GRAPH

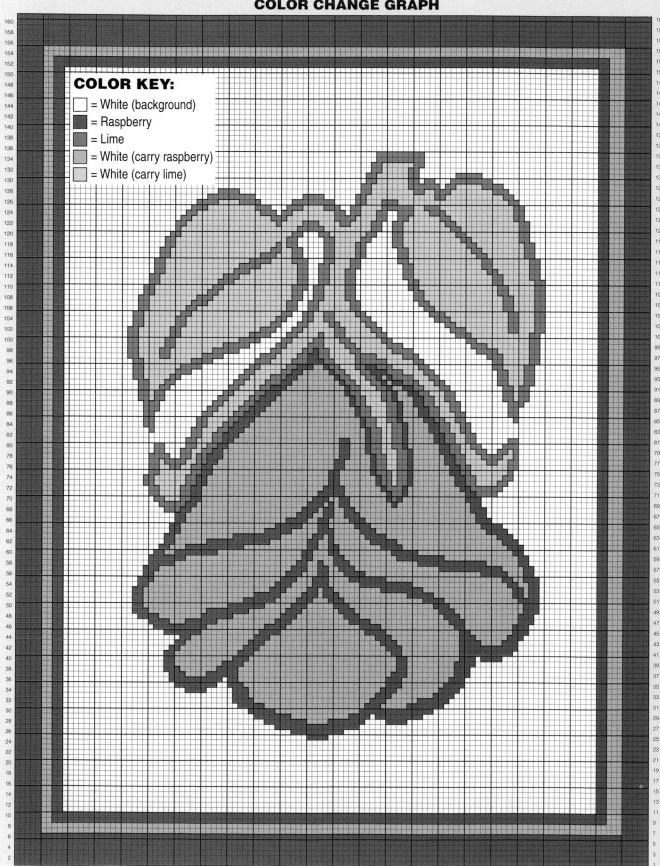

COLOR KEY:
- ☐ = White (background)
- ■ = Raspberry
- ■ = Lime
- ▨ = White (carry raspberry)
- ▨ = White (carry lime)

Flower Fantasy

Continued from page 56

Motif on last Row (see diagram), work same as First Row Second Large Motif.

Second Large Motif

Rnds 1-4: Repeat same rnds of First Large Motif on First Row.

Rnd 5: Working in opposite side of ch-10 on first petal, skip first 2 chs after joining sc of rnd 4, join dk. pink with sc in next ch, *sc in each of next 2 chs; working in ch-5 lps at ends of petals, shell in each of next 3 petals, sc in each of next 3 dc on same petal as last shell made, skip first 2 chs on opposite side of ch-10 on next petal, sc in next ch; repeat from *, sc in each of next 2 chs; joining to bottom of corresponding Large Motif on last Row made, [work joining shell in each of next 3 petals, sc in each of next 3 dc on same petal as last joining shell made], skip first 2 chs on opposite side of ch-10 on next petal, sc in each of next 3 chs; joining to side of last Large Motif made, repeat between [ ], join with sl st in first sc, fasten off.

Repeat Second Large Motif four more times for a total of six Motifs.

Repeat Second Row five more times for a total of seven Rows.

FILLER MOTIF

Rnds 1-2: Repeat same rnds of First Large Motif on First Row.

Rnd 3: Working this rnd in **back lps** only, join green with sc in any st, ch 3; working in open area between four joined Large Motifs, sc in ch-2 sp of shell at end of top right petal (see diagram), ch 3, skip next st on this Motif, sc in next st, [*ch 3, sc in ch-2 sp of shell at end of petal on next Large Motif, ch 3, skip next st on this Motif, sc in next st*, ch 5, sc in sp between 2 corner petals, ch 5, skip next st on this Motif, sc in next st; repeat between **]; repeat between [ ] 2 more times; repeat between **, ch 5, sc in sp between 2 corner petals,

ch 5, skip last st on this Motif, join, fasten off.

Repeat Filler Motif in each space between joined Large Motifs.

Edging

Working around entire outer edge, join green with sc in center ch sp of first shell at top right corner, *(ch 5, sc in center ch sp of next shell) 2 times, ch 5, sc in next ch sp on same shell, ch 5, sc in next corner sp between petals, ch 5, sc in first ch sp on next joined shell, ch 5, sc in joining between Motifs, ch 5, sc in last ch sp of same joined petal, ch 5, sc in corner sp between petals, ch 5, sc in first ch sp on next shell, ch 5, sc in center ch sp on same shell*; repeat between ** 4 more times, ◊(ch 5, sc in center ch sp on next shell) 2 times, ch 5, sc in last ch sp on same shell, ch 5, sc in corner sp between petals, ch 5, sc in first ch-2 sp on next shell, ch 5, sc in center ch sp on same shell◊; repeat between ** 6 more times; repeat between ◊◊; repeat between ** 5 more times; repeat between ◊◊; repeat between ** 6 more times, (ch 5, sc in center ch sp on next shell) 2 times, ch 5, sc in last ch sp on same shell, ch 5, sc in corner sp between petals, ch 5, sc in first ch-2 sp on next shell, ch 5, join with sl st in first sc, fasten off.

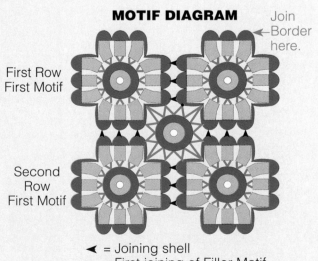

MOTIF DIAGRAM   Join Border here.

First Row First Motif

Second Row First Motif

◄ = Joining shell

• = First joining of Filler Motif

Library
Treasures

Cabled Lattice

Find peaceful solitude among the folds of this stately design stitched in starkly contrasting tones and a simple, yet distinctive, pattern.

Designed by
Maria Nagy

FINISHED SIZE
50" x 72".

MATERIALS
Worsted-weight yarn —
36 oz. off-white and
19 oz. blue; tapestry
needle; H crochet
hook or size needed
to obtain gauge.

GAUGE
7 dc = 2";
6 puff st rows = 5".

SKILL LEVEL
Easy

STRIP (make 10)
   Note: For **puff stitch (puff st),** yo, insert hook in next ch sp, yo, draw up long lp, (yo, insert hook in same sp, yo, draw up long lp) 3 times, yo, draw through all 9 lps on hook, ch 1.
   Row 1: With off-white, ch 8, sl st in first ch to form ring, ch 3, (puff st, ch 3, puff st, dc) in ring, turn (2 dc, 2 puff sts, 1 ch-3 sp).
   Rows 2-80: Ch 3, (puff st, ch 3, puff st) in next ch-3 sp, dc in last st, turn.
   Rnd 81: Working around outer edge, ch 3; for **shell,** (3 dc, ch 3, 3 dc) in next ch sp; working in ends of rows, dc in top of row 80, 2 dc around dc on same

row, (dc in top of next row, 2 dc around dc on same row) 79 times, dc in bottom of dc on row 1, shell in starting ring, dc in bottom of dc on row 1, 2 dc around dc on same row, (dc in top of same row, 2 dc around dc on next row) across, join with sl st in top of ch-3, fasten off.
   Rnd 82: Working in **back lps** only, join blue with sl st in first st, ch 3, *2 dc in each of next 3 sts, shell in next ch sp, 2 dc in each of next 3 sts, dc in each st across* to next shell; repeat between ******, join, fasten off.
   Leaving 18 sts on each end of Strips unworked, with blue, sew long edges together through **back lps.**

Geometrix

Old and new collide with magical precision in this invigorating art-nouveau rendition of an age-old art called crochet.

AFGHAN

Notes: At end of each row, **do not** turn, fasten off.

For **fringe,** ch 14 at beginning and end of each row.

Row 1: With white, for **starting ch,** ch 188, fasten off; fringe, sc in first ch on starting ch, sc in each ch across, fringe (188 sc, 2 fringe).

Row 2: With white, fringe, sc in **both lps** of first st, sc in **back lp** of each st across to last st, sc in **both lps** of last st, fringe.

Row 3: With black, fringe, sc in **both lps** of first st, sc in **back lp** of next st, *[dc in **front lp** of each of next 2 sts on row before last, sc in **back lp** of next st on last row, (dc in **front lp** of next st on row before last, sc in **back lp** of next st on last row) 4 times, dc in **front lp** of each of next 2 sts on row before last], sc in **back lp** of next 12 sts on last row, dc in **front lp** of each of next 2 sts on row before last, sc in **back lp** of next 16 sts on last row, dc in **front lp** of each of next 2 sts on row before last, sc in **back lp** of next 12 sts on last row; repeat from * 2 more times; repeat between [ ], sc in **back lp** of next st, sc in **both lps** of last st, fringe.

Notes: Each sc other than first and last sc will be worked in **back lp** of next st on last row unless otherwise stated.

Each dc will be worked in **front lp** of next st on row before last unless otherwise stated.

Row 4: With white, fringe, sc in **both lps** of first st, sc in next st, *[sc in each of next 2 sts, dc in next st, (sc in next st, dc in next st) 4 times, sc in each of next 2 sts], sc in next 11 sts, dc in next st, sc in each of next 2 sts, dc in next st, sc in next 14 sts, dc in next st, sc in each of next 2 sts, dc in next st, sc in next 11 sts; repeat from * 2 more times; repeat between [ ], sc in next st, sc in **both lps** of last st, fringe.

Row 5: With black, fringe, sc in **both lps** of first st, sc in next st, *[dc in each of next 2 sts, sc in next st, (dc in next st, sc in next st) 4 times, dc in each of next 2 sts], sc in next 10 sts, dc in next st, sc in next 4 sts, dc in next st, sc in next 12 sts, dc in next st, sc in next 4 sts, dc in next st, sc in next 10 sts; repeat from * 2 more times; repeat between [ ], sc in next st, sc in **both lps** of last st, fringe.

Row 6: With white, fringe, sc in **both lps** of first st, sc in next st, *[sc in each of next 2 sts, dc in next st, (sc in next st, dc in next st) 4 times, sc in each of next 2 sts], sc in next 9 sts, dc in next st,

Continued on page 76

Designed by
Kathleen D. Garen

FINISHED SIZE
45" x 62½"
not including fringe.

MATERIALS
Worsted-weight yarn —
29 oz. each black and
white; I crochet hook
or size needed to
obtain gauge.

GAUGE
3 sc = 1";
3 sc back lp rows = 1".

SKILL LEVEL
Challenging

Etched Copper

Glowing with a medley of burnished hues, the richly embossed surface of these post stitch blocks lets you revel in their warm texture and color.

BLOCK (make 63)

Rnd 1: With off-white, ch 5, sl st in first ch to form ring, ch 5, (3 dc in ring, ch 3) 3 times, 2 dc in ring, join with sl st in 3rd ch of ch 5 (12 dc, 4 ch sps).

Notes: For **long double crochet (ldc),** working over sts, yo, insert hook in ch sp on rnd before last, yo, draw up long lp, (yo, draw through 2 lps on hook) 2 times.

For **double crochet front post stitch (fp),** yo, insert hook from front to back around post of next st on rnd before last, yo, draw lp through, (yo, draw through 2 lps on hook) 2 times.

Rnd 2: Sl st in first ch sp, ch 5, dc in same sp, *[ldc in ring, dc in same sp as last dc on this rnd, skip next 3 sts], dc in next ch sp, ldc in ring, (dc, ch 3, dc) in same sp as last dc on this rnd; repeat from * 2 more times; repeat between [ ], dc in same sp as first ch-5, ldc in ring, join (16 dc, 8 ldc, 4 ch sps).

Rnd 3: Sl st in first ch sp, ch 5, dc in same sp, ldc in corresponding ch sp on rnd before last, *[dc in same sp as last dc on this rnd, skip next 3 sts, dc in sp between last st and next st, fp around 2nd dc of 3-dc group on rnd before last, dc in same sp as last dc on this rnd, skip next 3 sts], dc in

next ch sp, ldc in corresponding sp on rnd before last, (dc, ch 3, dc) in same sp as last dc on this rnd, ldc in same sp on rnd before last as last ldc; repeat from * 2 more times; repeat between [ ], dc in same sp as first ch-5, ldc in same sp on rnd before last, join, fasten off (24 dc, 8 ldc, 4 fp, 4 ch sps).

Rnd 4: Join peach with sl st in any ch sp, ch 5, dc in same sp, ldc in corresponding ch sp on rnd before last, *[dc in same sp as last dc on this rnd, skip next 3 sts, (dc in sp between last dc and next dc, fp around next ldc on rnd before last, dc in same sp as last dc on this rnd, skip next 3 sts) across to next ch sp], dc in next ch sp, ldc in corresponding sp on rnd before last, (dc, ch 3, dc) in same sp as last dc on this rnd, ldc in same sp on rnd before last as last ldc; repeat from * 2 more times; repeat between [ ], dc in same sp as first ch-5, ldc in corresponding sp on rnd before last, join.

Rnd 5: Sl st in next ch sp, ch 5, dc in same sp, ldc in corresponding sp on rnd before last, *[dc in same sp as last dc on this rnd, skip next 3 sts, (dc in sp between last dc and next dc, fp around next st on rnd before last, dc in

Designed by
Jeannine LaRoche

FINISHED SIZE
51" x 65".

MATERIALS
Worsted-weight yarn —
23 oz. dk. rust, 18 oz.
lt. rust, 13 oz. peach
and 8½ oz. off-white;
tapestry needle; H
crochet hook or size
needed to obtain gauge.

GAUGE
Rnds 1-3 = 2¾" across.
Each Block is 7" square.

SKILL LEVEL
Advanced

Continued on page 77

Plaited Ripple

Shifting lazily like dessert sands, layers of cross-stitches dance slowly back and forth to form a expressive, masculine throw.

Designed by
Susie Spier Maxfield

FINISHED SIZE
40" x 67".

MATERIALS
Worsted-weight yarn —
24 oz. each green and
off-white; H crochet
hook or size needed
to obtain gauge.

GAUGE
6 treble cross sts = 3½";
1 tr cross st row and 1
dc cross st row = 1¾".

SKILL LEVEL
Average

AFGHAN
Notes: For **treble crochet cross stitch (tr cr st)**, skip next ch or st, tr in next ch or st; working over last tr made, tr in skipped ch or st.

For **double crochet cross stitch (dc cr st),** skip next st, dc in next st; working over last dc made, dc in skipped st.

Row 1: With green, ch 207, 2 tr in 5th ch from hook, tr in next ch, *[tr cr st 5 times, skip next 4 chs, tr cr st 5 times], (2 tr, ch 3, 2 tr) in next ch; repeat from * 6 more times; repeat between [ ], tr in next st, 3 tr in last st, turn, fasten off.

Row 2: Join off-white with sl st in first st, ch 3, 2 dc in same st, dc in next st, *[dc cr st 5 times, skip next 4 sts, dc cr st 5 times], (2 dc, ch 3, 2 dc) in next ch sp; repeat from * 6 more times; repeat between [ ], dc in next st, 3 dc in last st, turn, fasten off.

Row 3: Join green with sl st in first st, ch 4, 2 tr in same st, tr in next st, *[tr cr st 5 times, skip next 4 sts, tr cr st 5 times], (2 tr, ch 3, 2 tr) in next ch sp; repeat from * 6 more times; repeat between [ ], tr in next st, 3 tr in last st, turn, fasten off.

Rows 4-61: Repeat rows 2 and 3 alternately.

Woven Fisherman

Understated sophistication and character abound in this traditional Aran design featuring cluster cables and a unique chain cross-stitch.

AFGHAN

Note: Beginning ch-2 or ch-3 is not used or counted as first st.

Row 1: Ch 126, hdc in 3rd ch from hook, hdc in each ch across, turn (124 hdc).

Row 2: Ch 2, hdc in each st across, turn.

Notes: For **cluster front post stitch (cl fp),** yo, insert hook from front to back around post of next st, yo, draw lp through, yo, draw through 2 lps on hook, yo, insert hook from front to back around post of same st, yo, draw lp through, yo, draw through 2 lps on hook, yo, draw through all 3 lps on hook.

For **cluster back post stitch (cl bp),** yo, insert hook from back to front around post of next st, yo, draw lp through, yo, draw through 2 lps on hook, yo, insert hook from back to front around post of same st, yo, draw lp through, yo, draw through 2 lps on hook, yo, draw through all 3 lps on hook.

For **cross stitch (cr st),** skip next st, insert hook in next st, yo, draw lp through; using first lp on hook, ch 2; yo, draw through both lps on hook; working behind last ch-2, dc in skipped st.

For **front post stitch (fp,** *see fig. 9, page 159),* yo, insert hook from front to back around post of next st, yo, draw lp through, (yo, draw through 2 lps on hook) 2 times.

For **back post stitch (bp),** yo, insert hook from back to front around post of next st, yo, draw lp through, (yo, draw through 2 lps on hook) 2 times.

Row 3: Ch 3, dc in **back lp** of first st, dc in **front lp** of next st, (dc in **back lp** of next st, dc in **front lp** of next st) 2 times, *cl fp around each of next 3 sts, cr st 10 times, cl fp around each of next 3 sts*, (skip next 2 sts, fp around next st; working behind fp, dc in each of last 2 skipped sts) 20 times; repeat between **, (dc in **back lp** of next st, dc in **front lp** of next st) 3 times, turn.

Row 4: Ch 3, dc in **front lp** of first st, dc in **back lp** of next st, (dc in **front lp** of next st, dc in **back lp** of next st) 2 times, *cl bp 3 times, cr st 10 times, cl bp 3 times*, (skip next 2 sts, bp around next st; working in front of bp, dc in each of last 2 skipped sts) 20 times; repeat between **, (dc in **front lp** of next st, dc in **back lp** of next st) 3 times, turn.

Rows 5-91: Repeat rows 3 and 4 alternately, ending with row 3.

Rows 92-93: Ch 2, hdc in each st across, turn. At end of last row, fasten off.

Continued on page 77

Designed by
Jennifer
Christiansen Simcik

FINISHED SIZE
45" x 60"
not including Fringe.

MATERIALS
Worsted-weight yarn —
57½ oz. aran; J crochet
hook or size needed
to obtain gauge.

GAUGE
11 dc = 4"; 8 cross st
rows = 5".

SKILL LEVEL
Advanced

Circles, Checks & Squares

Your favorite cowboy will love bedding down with this lively bandanna-inspired throw branded with colorful western flair.

Designed by
Ann E. Smith
*for Monsanto's
Designs for
America Program*

FINISHED SIZE
45½" x 60".

MATERIALS
Worsted-weight yarn —
29½ oz. black, 12½ oz.
red and 4 oz. white;
H crochet hook or size
needed to obtain gauge.

GAUGE
Rnd 1 of Square is 2"
across. Each Square
is 6½" square. Each
Block is 14½" square.

SKILL LEVEL
Average

BLOCK (make 12)
Square (make 4)

Rnd 1: With red, ch 6, sl st in first ch to form ring, ch 4, 23 tr in ring, join with sl st in top of ch-4, fasten off (24 tr).

Notes: When changing colors *(see fig. 11, page 159)*, work over dropped color and pick up as needed.

For **beginning V-stitch (beg V-st),** ch 5, dc in same st or sp.

For **V-stitch (V-st),** (dc, ch 2, dc) in next st or ch sp.

For **corner V-stitch (corner V-st),** dc in next ch sp, (ch 2, dc) 3 times in same sp.

Rnd 2: Working this rnd in **back lps** only, join black with sl st in first st, ch 3, dc in next st changing to white, 2 dc in next st changing to black in last st made, (dc in each of next 2 sts changing to white in last st made, 2 dc in next st changing to black in last st made) around, join with sl st in top of ch-3, fasten off white only (32 dc).

Rnd 3: Beg V-st, skip next st, (V-st in next st, skip next st) around, join with sl st in 3rd ch of ch-5 (16 V-sts).

Rnd 4: Sl st in first ch sp, beg V-st, V-st in each of next 2 ch sps, corner V-st, (V-st in each of next 3 ch sps, corner V-st) around, join (12 V-sts, 4 corner V-sts).

Rnd 5: Sl st in first ch sp, beg V-st, V-st in each of next 3 ch sps, corner V-st, (V-st in next 5 ch sps, corner V-st) 3 times, V-st in last ch sp, join, fasten off (20 V-sts, 4 corner V-sts).

To **join Squares,** with two Squares held right sides together, working through both thicknesses, join black with sl st in any corner ch sp, (ch 3, sl st in next ch sp) 8 times, ch 3; holding next 2 Squares right sides together, working through both thicknesses, sl st in any corner ch sp, (ch 3, sl st in next ch sp) 8 times, fasten off.

Join edges together at center in same manner to form one Block.

Edging

Working around Block, join red with sl st in any corner ch sp; for **beginning corner V-stitch (beg corner V-st),** ch 5, (dc, ch 2, dc, ch 2, dc) in same sp; (*V-st in next 7 ch sps, dc in next ch sp before seam, ch 2, dc in next ch sp after seam, V-st in next 7 ch sps*, corner V-st) 3 times; repeat

Continued on page 76

Circles, Checks & Squares

Continued from page 74

between **, join with sl st in 3rd ch of ch-5, fasten off.

To **join Blocks,** with two Blocks held right sides together, working through both thicknesses, join red with sl st in any corner ch sp, (ch 3, sl st in next ch sp) 18 times, *ch 3; holding next 2 Blocks right sides together, working through both thicknesses, sl st in any corner ch sp, (ch 3, sl st in next ch sp) 8 times; repeat from * across, fasten off.

Join Blocks in three rows of four Blocks each.

BORDER

Rnd 1: Join red with sc in corner ch sp before one short end, 2 sc in same sp, (evenly space 156 more sc across to next corner ch sp, 3 sc in next corner ch sp, evenly space 212 sc across to next corner ch sp), 3 sc in next corner ch sp; repeat between ( ), join with sl st in first sc, fasten off (156 sc on each short end between corner 3-sc groups, 212 sc on each long edge between corner 3-sc groups).

Note: Always change to next color in last st of last color used.

Rnd 2: Join black with sl st in first st of any corner 3-sc group before one short end, ch 3, dc in same st; *with white, 2 dc in next st; with black, 2 dc in next st; (with white, dc in each of next 2 sts; with black, dc in each of next 2 sts) across to next corner 3-sc group; with white, 2 dc in next st; with black, 2 dc in next st; with white, 2 dc in next st; (with black, dc in each of next 2 sts; with white, dc in each of next 2 sts) across* to next corner 3-sc group; with black, 2 dc in next st; repeat between **, join with sl st in top of ch-3, **turn,** fasten off.

Rnd 3: Join black with sl st in first st, sl st in each st around, join with sl st in first sl st, fasten off.

Geometrix

Continued from page 67

sc in next 6 sts, dc in next st, sc in next 10 sts, dc in next st, sc in next 6 sts, dc in next st, sc in next 9 sts; repeat from * 2 more times; repeat between [ ], sc in next st, sc in **both lps** of last st, fringe.

Row 7: With black, fringe, sc in **both lps** of first st, sc in next st, *[dc in each of next 2 sts, sc in next st, (dc in next st, sc in next st) 4 times, dc in each of next 2 sts], sc in next 8 sts, (dc in next st, sc in next 8 sts) 4 times; repeat from * 2 more times; repeat between [ ], sc in next st, sc in **both lps** of last st, fringe.

Row 8: With white, fringe, sc in **both lps** of first st, sc in next st, *[sc in each of next 2 sts, dc in next st, (sc in next st, dc in next st) 4 times, sc in each of next 2 sts], dc in next st, sc in next 6 sts, dc in next st, (sc in next 10 sts, dc in next st, sc in next 6 sts, dc in next st) 2 times; repeat from * 2 more times; repeat between [ ], sc in next st, sc in **both lps** of last st, fringe.

Row 9: With black, fringe, sc in **both lps** of first st, sc in next st, *[dc in each of next 2 sts, sc in next st, (dc in next st, sc in next st) 4 times, dc in each of next 2 sts], sc in next st, dc in next st, sc in next 4 sts, dc in next st, (sc in next 12 sts, dc in next st, sc in next 4 sts, dc in next st) 2 times, sc in next st; repeat from * 2 more times; repeat between [ ], sc in next st, sc in **both lps** of last st, fringe.

Row 10: With white, fringe, sc in **both lps** of first st, sc in next st, *[sc in each of next 2 sts, dc in next st, (sc in next st, dc in next st) 4 times, sc in each of next 2 sts], dc in next st, sc in next st, dc in next st, sc in each of next 2 sts, dc in next st, (sc in next 14 sts, dc in next st, sc in each of next 2 sts, dc in next st) 2 times, sc in next st, dc in next st; repeat from * 2 more times; repeat between [ ], sc in next st, sc in **both**

lps of last st, fringe.

Row 11: With black, fringe, sc in **both lps** of first st, sc in next st, *[dc in each of next 2 sts, sc in next st, (dc in next st, sc in next st) 4 times, dc in each of next 2 sts], sc in next st, dc in next st, sc in next st, dc in each of next 2 sts, (sc in next 16 sts, dc in each of next 2 sts) 2 times, sc in next st, dc in next st, sc in next st; repeat from * 2 more times; repeat between [ ], sc in next st, sc in **both lps** of last st, fringe.

Row 12: Repeat row 10.

Row 13: Repeat row 9.

Row 14: Repeat row 8.

Row 15: Repeat row 7.

Row 16: Repeat row 6.

Row 17: Repeat row 5.

Row 18: Repeat row 4.

Rows 19-132: Repeat rows 3-18 consecutively, ending with row 4.

Row 133: Fringe, sc in each st across, fringe.

Row 134: Skip fringe, join with sl st in first st, sl st in each st across, **do not** fringe.

Row 135: Working in starting ch on opposite side of row 1, fringe, join white with sl st in first ch, sl st in each ch across, fringe.✍

Etched Copper
Continued from page 69

same sp as last dc on this rnd, skip next 3 sts) across to next ch sp], dc in next ch sp, ldc in corresponding sp on rnd before last, (dc, ch 3, dc) in same sp as last dc on this rnd, ldc in same sp on rnd before last as last ldc; repeat from * 2 more times; repeat between [ ], dc in same sp as first ch-5, ldc in corresponding sp on rnd before last, join, fasten off.

Rnds 6-7: With lt. rust, repeat rnds 4 and 5.

Rnds 8-9: With dk. rust, repeat rnds 4 and 5, ending with 27 sts between each corner ch sp on last rnd.

Matching sts, with dk. rust, sew Blocks together in seven rows of nine Blocks each.

BORDER

Rnd 1: Working around outer edge, join peach with sc in any corner ch sp, 2 sc in same sp, [◊sc in each of next 3 sts, (skip next st, sc in each of next 3 sts) 6 times, *sc in next ch sp, skip next seam, sc in next ch sp, sc in each of next 3 sts, (skip next st, sc in each of next 3 sts) 6 times; repeat from * across◊ to next corner ch sp, 3 sc in next ch sp]; repeat between [ ] 2 times; repeat between ◊◊, join with sl st in first sc, **turn.**

Note: For **single crochet back post stitch (sc bp),** insert hook from back to front around post of next st, complete as sc.

Rnd 2: Ch 1, sc bp around each st around, join, **turn,** fasten off.

Rnd 3: Join lt. rust with sc in first st, sc in same st, 2 sc in each of next 2 sts, (sc in each st across to 3 sts at next corner, 2 sc in each of next 3 sts) 3 times, sc in each st across, join, turn.

Rnd 4: Repeat rnd 2.

Rnds 5-6: With dk. rust, repeat rnds 3 and 4.✍

Woven Fisherman
Continued from page 73

FRINGE

For **each Fringe,** cut three strands each 13" long. With all strands held together, fold in half, insert hook in st, draw fold through st, draw all loose ends through fold, tighten. Trim ends.

Fringe in every other st on short ends of Afghan.✍

Hospitality Suites

Lilac Time

Tempt friends and loved ones to stay a while longer with this lavishly thick throw that's sure to warm their hearts as well as their toes.

Designed by
Daisy Watson

FINISHED SIZE
57" x 79".

MATERIALS
Worsted-weight yarn —
69 oz. lilac; J crochet
hook or size needed to
obtain gauge.

GAUGE
5 dc = 2"; 3 dc rows = 2".

SKILL LEVEL
Average

AFGHAN

Row 1: Ch 197, hdc in 3rd ch from hook, hdc in each ch across, turn (196 hdc).

Row 2: Ch 3, dc in each st across, turn.

Notes: For **double treble crochet (dtr),** yo 3 times, insert hook in next st, yo, draw lp through, (yo, draw through 2 lps on hook) 4 times.

For **back zigzag stitch (bzs),** skip next 3 sts, dtr in next st; working in front of dtr just made, dc in first skipped st, dc in each of next 2 skipped sts.

For **front zigzag stitch (fzs)**, skip next 3 sts, dtr in next st; working behind dtr just made, dc in first skipped st, dc in each of next 2 skipped sts.

Row 3: Ch 3, dc in next st, fzs across to last 2 sts, dc in each of last 2 sts, turn (48 fzs, 4 dc).

Row 4: Ch 3, dc in next st, bzs across to last 2 sts, dc in each of last 2 sts, turn.

Row 5: Ch 3, dc in each st across, turn (196 dc).

Note: For **puff stitch (puff st),** (yo, insert hook in same st, yo, draw up ¾"-long lp) 3 times, yo, draw through 6 lps on hook, yo, draw through last 2 lps on hook.

Row 6: Ch 2, (hdc, puff st) in next st, *skip next st, (sc, puff st) in next st; repeat from * across to last 2 sts, hdc in each of last 2 sts, turn (97 puff sts, 96 sc, 4 hdc).

Row 7: Ch 2, hdc in next st, skip next puff st, *(sc, puff st) in next sc, skip next puff st; repeat from * across to last 2 sts, hdc in each of last 2 sts, turn (96 puff sts, 96 sc, 4 hdc).

Rows 8-95: Repeat rows 2-7 consecutively, ending with row 5.

Row 96: Ch 2, hdc in each st across, turn.

Rnd 97: Working in sts and in ends of rows around outer edge, ch 1, [(2 sc, ch 3, 2 sc) in first st, sc in each of next 2 sts, *(sc, ch 3, sc) in next st, sc in each of next 2 sts*; repeat between ** across to last st, (2 sc, ch 3, 2 sc) in last st, skip first row, 2 sc in next row, ◊(sc, ch 3, sc) in next row, 2 sc in next row, (sc, ch 3, sc) in next row, sc in each of next 2 rows; repeat from ◊ across to last 4 rows, (sc, ch 3, sc) in next row, 2 sc in next row, (sc, ch 3, sc) in next row, sc in last row]; working in opposite side of starting ch on row 1, repeat between [ ], join with sl st in first sc, fasten off.

Medley in Blue

The perfect accompaniment to breakfast in bed, guests will feel especially pampered when they find this spirited cover near their tray.

BLOCK (make 30)

Rnd 1: With white, ch 6, sl st in first ch to form ring, ch 3, 15 dc in ring, join with sl st in top of ch-3 (16 dc).

Rnd 2: Ch 8, dc in same st, *[ch 1, (dc in next st, ch 1) 3 times], (dc, ch 5, dc) in next st; repeat from * 2 more times; repeat between [ ], join with sl st in 3rd ch of ch-8, fasten off (20 dc, 20 ch sps).

Notes: For **beginning popcorn (beg pc),** ch 3, 3 dc in same st, drop lp from hook, insert hook in top of ch-3, pick up dropped lp, draw through st.

For **popcorn (pc),** 4 dc in next st, drop lp from hook, insert hook in first st of 4-dc group, pick up dropped lp, draw through st.

Rnd 3: Join lt. blue with sl st in any corner ch-5 sp, beg pc, ch 5, pc in same sp, *[ch 1, (pc in next ch sp, ch 1) across] to next corner ch-5 sp, (pc, ch 5, pc) in corner ch sp; repeat from * 2 more times; repeat between [ ], join with sl st in top of beg pc, fasten off (24 pc, 24 ch sps).

Rnd 4: With med. blue, repeat rnd 3 (28 pc, 28 ch sps).

Notes: For **beginning shell (beg shell),** ch 3, (2 dc, ch 3, 3 dc) in same sp.

For **shell,** (3 dc, ch 3, 3 dc) in next ch sp.

Rnd 5: Join dk. blue with sl st in any corner ch-5 sp, beg shell, 3 dc in each ch sp around with shell in each corner ch sp, join with sl st in top of ch-3, fasten off (24 3-dc groups, 4 shells).

Rnd 6: Join white with sl st in any corner ch sp, beg shell, dc in each st around with shell in each corner ch sp, join (96 dc, 4 shells).

Rnd 7: Ch 3, dc in each st around with (dc, ch 3, dc) in each corner ch sp, fasten off (128 dc, 4 ch sps).

Rnd 8: Join lt. blue with sl st in any corner ch sp, ch 4, pc in same sp, *[ch 2, skip next 2 sts, (pc in next st, ch 2, skip next 2 sts) across] to next corner ch sp, (pc, ch 4, pc) in corner ch sp; repeat from * 2 more times; repeat between [ ], join with sl st in top of beg pc, fasten off (48 pc, 48 ch sps).

Rnd 9: Join med. blue with sl st in any corner ch sp, beg pc, ch 4, pc in same sp, *[ch 2, (pc in next ch sp, ch 2) across] to next corner ch sp, (pc, ch 4, pc) in corner ch sp; repeat from * 2 more times; repeat between [ ], join, fasten off (52 pc, 52 ch sps).

Rnd 10: Repeat rnd 5 (48 3-dc groups, 4 shells).

Matching sts and ch sps, with dk. blue, sew Blocks together

Continued on page 95

Designed by
Rosetta Harshman

FINISHED SIZE
57" x 67".

MATERIALS
Worsted-weight yarn —
29 oz. white, 9 oz.
each lt., med. and dk.
blue; tapestry needle;
F crochet hook or size
needed to obtain gauge.

GAUGE
9 dc = 2"; Rnds 1-2 of
Block = 3" across.
Each Block is
10½" square.

SKILL LEVEL
Average

Shifting Sapphires

Reflected over and over as if through the facets of a jewel, the opulent array of colors in this design make it a splendid addition to your decor.

AFGHAN

Row 1: With med. blue, ch 195, dc in 4th ch from hook, dc in each of next 3 chs, (dc, ch 1, dc) in next ch, dc in next 5 chs, *skip next 2 chs, dc in next 5 chs, (dc, ch 1, dc) in next ch, dc in next 5 chs; repeat from * across, turn (180 dc, 15 ch-1 sps).

Rows 2-3: Ch 3, skip next st, dc in next 4 sts, (dc, ch 1, dc) in next ch-1 sp, *dc in next 5 sts, skip next 2 sts, dc in next 5 sts, (dc, ch 1, dc) in next ch-1 sp; repeat from * across to last 6 sts, dc in next 4 sts, skip next st, dc in last st, turn. At end of last row, fasten off.

Row 4: Join lt. blue with sl st in first st, ch 3, skip next st, dc in next 4 sts, (dc, ch 1, dc) in next ch-1 sp, *dc in next 5 sts, skip next 2 sts, dc in next 5 sts, (dc, ch 1, dc) in next ch-1 sp; repeat from * across to last 6 sts, dc in next 4 sts, skip next st, dc in last st, turn.

Rows 5-6: Repeat rows 2 and 3.

Row 7: With lilac, repeat row 4.

Rows 8-9: Repeat rows 2 and 3.

Row 10: With lavender, repeat row 4.

Rows 11-12: Repeat rows 2 and 3.

Row 13: With med. blue, repeat row 4.

Rows 14-123: Repeat rows 2-13 consecutively, ending with row 3.

Designed by
Fran Hetchler

FINISHED SIZE
50" x 74".

MATERIALS
Worsted-weight yarn —
15 oz. each med. blue,
lt. blue, purple and
lavender; H crochet
hook or size needed to
obtain gauge.

GAUGE
7 dc = 2"; 5 dc rows = 3".

SKILL LEVEL
Easy

Grapevine Lace

Inviting strands of luscious-looking clusters add distinctive gourmet flavor to any room and any style from traditional to country.

Designed by
Katherine Eng

FINISHED SIZE
42" x 60".

MATERIALS
Worsted-weight yarn —
16 oz. med. green,
11 oz. violet, 9 oz. dk.
green and 7 oz. dk.
pink; H crochet hook
or size needed to
obtain gauge.

GAUGE
Rnd 1 is 58¼" long.
Each Strip is 5¼" wide.

SKILL LEVEL
Average

FIRST STRIP

Rnd 1: With med. green, ch 197, (sc, ch 2, sc, ch 3, sc, ch 2, sc) in 2nd ch from hook, [ch 1, skip next 2 chs, *(sc, ch 2, sc) in next ch, ch 1, skip next 2 chs; repeat from * across] to last ch, (sc, ch 2, sc, ch 3, sc, ch 2, sc) in last ch; working on opposite side of starting ch, repeat between [ ], join with sl st in first sc, fasten off (264 sc).

Notes: For **beginning cluster (beg cl),** ch 3, (yo, insert hook in same sp, yo, draw lp through, yo, draw through 2 lps on hook) 2 times, yo, draw through all 3 lps on hook.

For **cluster (cl),** yo, insert hook in next ch sp, yo, draw lp through, yo, draw through 2 lps on hook, (yo, insert hook in same sp, yo, draw lp through, yo, draw through 2 lps on hook) 2 times, yo, draw through all 4 lps on hook.

Rnd 2: Join violet with sl st in ch-3 sp on either end, beg cl, *(ch 2, cl, ch 3, cl, ch 2, cl) in same sp, ch 2, cl in next ch-2 sp, (ch 2, skip next ch-1 sp, cl in next ch-2 sp) across* to ch-3 sp on other end, ch 2, cl in next ch-3 sp; repeat between **, ch 2, join with sl st in beg cl, fasten off.

Rnd 3: Join green with sc in ch-3 sp on either end, [(ch 2, sc, ch 3, sc, ch 2, sc) in same sp, ch 1, *(sc, ch 2, sc) in next ch sp, ch 1; repeat from * across] to ch-3 sp on other end, sc in next ch sp; repeat between [ ], join with sl st in first sc, fasten off.

Notes: For **shell,** (2 dc, ch 2, 2 dc) in next ch sp.

For **end shell,** (3 dc, ch 3, 3 dc) in next ch sp.

Rnd 4: Join med. green with sc in 5th ch sp before ch-3 sp on either end, *ch 1, skip next ch sp, shell in next ch sp, ch 1, skip next ch sp, sc in next ch sp, end shell in next ch-3 sp, sc in next ch sp, ch 1, skip next ch sp, shell in next ch sp, ch 1, skip next ch sp, (sc in next ch sp, skip next ch sp, shell in next ch sp, skip next ch sp) across* to 5 ch sps before ch-3 sp on other end, sc in next ch sp; repeat between **, join, fasten off.

Rnd 5: Join dk. pink with sc in first sc of last rnd, [ch 3, sc in same sc, ch 3, (sc, ch 3, sc) in ch sp of next shell, ch 3, (sc, ch 3, sc) in next sc, ch 3, (sc, ch 3, sc, ch 4, sc, ch 3, sc) in ch sp of end shell, ch 3, (sc, ch 3, sc) in next sc, ch 3, (sc, ch 3, sc) in ch sp of next shell, ch 3, (sc, ch 3, sc) in next sc, ch 2, (sc, ch 4, sc) in ch sp of next shell, ch 2, *sc in next sc, ch 2, (sc, ch 4, sc) in ch sp of next shell, ch 2; repeat from * 31

Continued on page 95

Rosewood Elegance

Envision a room emminating with the exquisite charm of fine polished woods and leather, then complete the scene with this exceptional afghan.

AFGHAN

Notes: For **shell,** 5 dc in next st or ch.

For **beginning half shell (beg half shell),** ch 3, 2 dc in same st.

For **end half shell,** 3 dc in last ch or st.

For **reverse shell (rev shell),** (yo, insert hook in next st or ch, yo, draw lp through, yo, draw through 2 lps on hook) 5 times, yo, draw through all 6 lps on hook, ch 1.

Front of row 1 is wrong side of work.

Row 1: With burgundy, ch 166, 2 dc in 4th ch from hook, skip next 2 chs, sc in next ch, skip next 2 chs, (shell in next ch, skip next 2 chs, sc in next ch, skip next 2 chs) across to last ch, end half shell, turn, fasten off (27 sc, 26 shells, 2 half shells).

Row 2: Join lt. green with sc in first st, (ch 2, rev shell, ch 2, sc in next st) across, turn (28 sc, 27 rev shells).

Row 3: Beg half shell, sc in next rev shell, (shell in next sc, sc in next rev shell) across to last sc, end half shell, turn, fasten off.

Rows 4-5: With burgundy, repeat rows 2 and 3.

Rows 6-7: With pink, repeat rows 2 and 3.

Rows 8-9: With burgundy, repeat rows 2 and 3.

Rows 10-124: Repeat rows 2-9 consecutively, ending with row 4. At end of last row, fasten off.

FRINGE

For **each Fringe,** cut five strands burgundy each 16" long. With all strands held together, fold in half, insert hook in st, draw fold through, draw all loose ends through fold, tighten. Trim ends.

Fringe in each rev shell and in each sc on last row of Afghan; fringe in base of each shell and in each sc on row 1.

Designed by Dorris Brooks

FINISHED SIZE
47½" x 67"
not including Fringe.

MATERIALS
Worsted-weight yarn —
34 oz. burgundy, 17 oz. lt. green and 13 oz. pink; H crochet hook or size needed to obtain gauge.

GAUGE
4 shells and 4 sc = 7";
3 shell rows and
3 sc rows = 3¼".

SKILL LEVEL
Average

Vanilla Delight

For those who enjoy the finer things in life comes an unforgettable creation of refined taste and timeless appeal.

Designed by
Katherine Eng

FINISHED SIZE
39" x 61".

MATERIALS
Worsted-weight yarn —
36 oz. off-white;
H crochet hook or
size needed to
obtain gauge.

GAUGE
7 dc = 2". Each Strip
is 5½" wide.

SKILL LEVEL
Average

FIRST STRIP
   Rnd 1: Ch 190, dc in 4th ch from hook, dc in each ch across to last ch, (3 dc, ch 3, 3 dc) in last ch; working on opposite side of ch, dc in each ch across, (3 dc, ch 3, dc) in same ch as first st, join with sl st in top of ch-3 (382 dc, 2 ch sps).
   Note: For **front post stitch (fp,** *see fig. 9, page 159)*, yo, insert hook from front to back around post of next st on rnd before last, yo, draw lp through, (yo, draw through 2 lps on hook) 2 times.
   Rnd 2: Sl st in next st, ch 3, *(fp, dc in next st) across to next ch sp, (3 dc, ch 3, 3 dc) in next ch sp, dc in next st; repeat from *, fp, join with sl st in top of ch-3 (394 sts, 2 ch sps).
   Rnd 3: Ch 1, sc in first st, *[ch 1, skip next st, (sc in next st, ch 1, skip next st) across] to next ch sp, (sc, ch 1, sc, ch 2, sc, ch 1, sc) in next ch sp; repeat from *; repeat between [ ], join with sl st in first sc.
   Notes: For **beginning cluster (beg cl),** ch 3, (yo, insert hook in same sp, yo, draw lp through, yo, draw through 2 lps on hook) 2 times, yo, draw through all 3 lps on hook.
   For **cluster (cl),** yo, insert hook in next ch sp, yo, draw lp through, yo, draw through 2 lps on hook, (yo, insert hook in same sp, yo,

draw lp through, yo, draw through 2 lps on hook) 2 times, yo, draw through all 4 lps on hook.
   Rnd 4: Sl st in first ch-1 sp, beg cl, *[ch 1, (cl in next ch-1 sp, ch 1) across] to ch-2 sp on next end, (cl, ch 3, cl) in next ch-2 sp; repeat from *; repeat between [ ], join with sl st in top of beg cl.
   Rnd 5: Sl st in first ch-1 sp, ch 1, sc in same sp, *[ch 1, (sc in next ch-1 sp, ch 1) across] to ch-3 sp on next end, (sc, ch 1, sc, ch 2, sc, ch 1, sc) in next ch-3 sp; repeat from *; repeat between [ ], join with sl st in first sc.
   Rnd 6: Sl st in first ch-1 sp, ch 1, (sc, ch 3, sc) in same sp, (sc, ch 3, sc) in each ch-1 sp around with (sc, ch 3, sc, ch 3, sc, ch 3, sc) in ch-2 sp at each end, join (216 ch-3 sps).
   Rnd 7: Sl st in first ch sp, ch 1, sc in same sp, ch 1, [*(sc, ch 3, sc) in next ch sp, ch 1, sc in next ch sp, ch 1; repeat from * across to 8 ch sps before center ch-3 sp on next end], (sc, ch 3, sc, ch 1) in next 16 ch sps; repeat between [ ], (sc, ch 3, sc, ch 1) in each ch sp across, join, fasten off.

REMAINING STRIPS (make 5)
   Rnds 1-6: Repeat same rnds of First Strip.
   Rnd 7: Sl st in first ch sp, ch 1,

Continued on page 95

Flight of Fancy

Let your troubles take wing and soar away with this light as a breeze one-piece spread worked in easy single crochet stitches.

Designed by
Rhonda Simpson

FINISHED SIZE
56" x 65".

MATERIALS
Worsted-weight yarn —
29 oz. white, 12 oz.
dk. rose, 9 oz. each lt.
rose and dk. blue,
7 oz. lt. blue; K crochet
hook or size needed
to obtain gauge.

GAUGE
9 sc = 4"; 5 sc rows = 2".

SKILL LEVEL
Average

AFGHAN
Row 1: With white, ch 108, sc in 2nd ch from hook, sc in each ch across, turn (107 sc).

Rows 2-11: Ch 1, sc in each st across, turn.

Notes: When changing colors *(see fig. 11, page 159)*, always drop yarn to wrong side of work. Use a separate skein of yarn for each color section. **Do not** carry yarn across from one section to another. Fasten off colors at end of each color section.

Work odd-numbered graph rows from left to right and even-numbered rows from right to left.

Row 12: For row 12 of graph, ch 1, sc in first 13 sts changing to med. blue in last st made, sc in next 6 sts changing to white in last st made, sc in each st across, turn.

Rows 13-129: Ch 1, sc in each st across changing colors accord-ing to graph, turn.

Rows 130-140: With white, ch 1, sc in each st across, turn. At end of last row, **do not** fasten off.

BORDER
Rnd 1: Working around outer edge, with wrong side of work facing you, ch 1, sc in each st and in end of each row around with 3 sc in each corner, join with sl st in first sc, **turn,** fasten off.

Rnd 2: Join lt. rose with sc in any st, sc in each st around with 3 sc in each center corner st, join, **turn.**

Rnds 3-5: Ch 1, sc in each st around with 3 sc in each center corner st, join, **turn.** At end of last rnd, fasten off.

Rnds 6-7: With white, repeat rnds 2 and 3. At end of last rnd, fasten off.

Rnds 8-11: With lt. blue, repeat rnds 2-5.

Graph on page 94

Flight of Fancy

Instructions on page 92

COLOR KEY:

- = Dk. Blue
- = Lt. Blue
- = Dk. Rose
- = Lt. Rose
- = White

COLOR CHANGE GRAPH

Medley in Blue

Continued from page 83

through **back lps** only in five rows of six Blocks each.

BORDER

Rnd 1: Working around outer edge, join dk. blue with sl st in any corner ch sp, beg shell, *[dc in each st, in each joined ch sp and in each seam across] to next corner ch sp, shell in corner ch sp; repeat from * 2 more times; repeat between [ ], join with sl st in top of ch-3, fasten off.

Rnd 2: Join white with sl st in any st, ch 2, hdc in each st around with (3 hdc, ch 3, 3 hdc) in each corner ch sp, join with sl st in top of ch-2, fasten off.

Rnd 3: Join lt. blue with sl st in any st, hdc in each st around with 3 hdc in each corner ch sp, join, fasten off.

Rnd 4: Join med. blue with sl st in any st, hdc in each st around with 3 hdc in each center corner st, join, fasten off.

Rnd 5: With dk. blue, repeat rnd 4.

Grapevine Lace

Continued from page 86

more times], sc in next sc; repeat between [ ], join, fasten off.

SECOND STRIP

Rnds 1-4: Repeat same rnds of First Strip.

Rnd 5: Join dk. pink with sc in first sc of last rnd, [ch 3, sc in same sc, ch 3, (sc, ch 3, sc) in ch sp of next shell, ch 3, (sc, ch 3, sc) in next sc, ch 3, (sc, ch 3, sc, ch 4, sc, ch 3, sc) in ch sp of end shell, ch 3, (sc, ch 3, sc) in next sc, ch 3, (sc, ch 3, sc) in ch sp of next shell, ch 3, (sc, ch 3, sc) in next sc, ch 2], (sc, ch 4, sc) in ch sp of next shell, ch 2, *sc in next sc, ch 2, (sc, ch 4, sc) in ch sp of next shell, ch 2; repeat from * 31 more times, sc in next sc; repeat between [ ], sc in ch sp of next shell, ch 2; to **join Strips,** sl st in corresponding ch sp on last Strip made, ch 2, sc in same sp on this Strip, ch 2, ◊sc in next sc, ch 2, sc in ch sp of next shell, ch 2, sl st in corresponding ch sp on last Strip made, ch 2, sc in same sp on this Strip, ch 2; repeat from ◊ 31 more times, join, fasten off.

Repeat Second Strip six more times for a total of eight Strips.

Vanilla Delight

Continued from page 90

sc in same sp, ch 1, *(sc, ch 3, sc) in next ch sp, ch 1, sc in next ch sp, ch 1; repeat from * across to 8 ch sps before center ch-3 sp on next end, (sc, ch 3, sc, ch 1) in next 16 ch sps; to **join Strips,** holding this Strip and last Strip made wrong sides together, sc in next ch sp on this Strip, ch 1, sl st in corresponding ch sp on last Strip made, ch 1, sc in same sp on this Strip, ch 1, (sc in next ch sp, ch 1, sc in next ch sp, ch 1, sl st in next ch sp on last Strip made, ch 1, sc in same sp on this Motif, ch 1) 46 times, (sc, ch 3, sc, ch 1) in each ch sp across, join, fasten off.

Sweet Dreams
Nursery

Quilted Pastels

Fresh-as-spring colors blended with pristine white let you shower the newest addition to your family with a rainbow of love.

BLOCK (make 20)

Rnd 1: With white, ch 4, sl st in first ch to form ring, ch 1, 8 sc in ring, join with sl st in first sc (8 sc).

Rnd 2: For **beginning cluster (cl),** ch 3, (yo, insert hook in same st, yo, draw lp through, yo, draw through 2 lps on hook) 2 times, yo, draw through all 3 lps on hook; ch 3; *for **cluster (cl),** yo, insert hook in next st, yo, draw lp through, yo, draw through 2 lps on hook, (yo, insert hook in same st, yo, draw lp through, yo, draw through 2 lps on hook) 2 times, yo, draw through all 4 lps on hook; ch 3; repeat from * around, join with sl st in top of beg cl, fasten off (8 cls, 8 ch-3 sps).

Rnd 3: Join mint with sc in any ch-3 sp, sc in same sp, (2 sc, ch 2, 2 sc) in each of next 7 ch-3 sps, 2 sc in same sp as first sc; **to join,** hdc in first sc (8 ch-2 sps).

Note: For **large shell,** (3 dc, ch 2, 3 dc) in next ch sp.

Rnd 4: Ch 1, sc around joining hdc, ch 2, large shell in next ch sp, ch 2, (sc in next ch sp, ch 2, large shell in next ch sp, ch 2) around, join with sl st in first sc, fasten off (8 ch-2 sps, 4 large shells, 4 sc).

Rnd 5: Join white with sc in ch sp of any large shell, ch 3, sc in same sp, *[sc in each of next 3 sts, 2 sc in next ch sp, sc in next st, 2 sc in next ch sp, sc in each of next 3 sts], (sc, ch 3, sc) in next ch sp;

repeat from * 2 more times; repeat between [ ], join, fasten off (13 sc between each corner ch sp).

Row 6: For **first triangle,** working in rows, join pink with sc in any corner ch sp, ch 1, skip next st, (sc in next st, ch 1, skip next st) 6 times, sc in next ch sp leaving remaining sts unworked, turn (8 sc, 7 ch-1 sps).

Rows 7-10: Ch 1, sc first st and next ch sp tog, ch 1, (sc in next ch sp, ch 1) across to last ch sp, sc next ch sp and last st tog, turn, ending with 4 sc and 3 ch-1 sps in last row.

Row 11: Ch 1, sc first st and next ch sp tog, ch 1, sc in next ch sp, ch 1, sc next ch sp and last st tog, turn (3 sc, 2 ch-1 sps).

Row 12: Ch 1, sc first st and next ch-1 sp tog, ch 1, sc next ch-1 sp and last st tog, turn (2 sc, 1 ch-1 sp).

Row 13: Ch 1, sc in first st, ch 1, skip next ch-1 sp, sc in last st, turn, fasten off.

Row 6: For **second triangle,** join lilac with sc in same ch sp as last sc of first row on last triangle made, ch 1, skip next st, (sc in next st, ch 1, skip next st) 6 times, sc in next ch sp leaving remaining sts unworked, turn.

Rows 7-13: Repeat same rows of first triangle.

Continued on page 105

Designed by Katherine Eng

FINISHED SIZE
34" x 41".

MATERIALS
Worsted-weight yarn — 13 oz. white, 7 oz. mint, 2 oz. each lilac, pink, yellow and blue; tapestry needle; G crochet hook or size needed to obtain gauge.

GAUGE
4 sc = 1"; 4 sc rows = 1". Each Block is 7" square.

SKILL LEVEL
Average

Tender Innocence

Fondly remember the past as you warmly embrace the future with a delicate design inspired by the old-fashioned granny square.

Designed by
Pamela J. McKee

FINISHED SIZE
28" x 35".

MATERIALS
Fuzzy baby yarn —
14½ oz. pink, 3½ oz.
yellow and 2 oz. white;
tapestry needle; D and
E crochet hooks or
sizes needed to
obtain gauges.

GAUGE
D hook, 5 sc = 1". E
hook, rnds 1-2 of
Motif = 2" across. Each
Motif is 3¾" square.

SKILL LEVEL
Average

MOTIF (make 63, see Note)
Note: Make 40 Motifs using yellow on rnd 2; make 23 using white on rnd 2.
Rnd 1: With E hook and pink, ch 5, sl st in first ch to form ring, ch 5, (dc in ring, ch 2) 7 times, join with sl st in 3rd ch of ch-5, fasten off (8 dc, 8 ch-2 sps).
Note: For **popcorn (pc),** 4 dc in next st, drop lp from hook, insert hook in first st of 4-dc group, pick up dropped lp, draw through st.
Rnd 2: Join yellow or white with sl st in any st, ch 4, dc in same st, ch 1, pc in next ch sp, ch 1, *(dc, ch 1, dc) in next st, ch 1, pc in next ch sp, ch 1; repeat from * around, join with sl st in 3rd ch of ch-4, fasten off (24 ch-1 sps, 16 dc, 8 pc).
Rnd 3: Join pink with sl st in first st, ch 3, *[(2 dc, ch 3, 2 dc) in next ch sp, dc in next dc, ch 1, skip next pc, hdc in next dc, hdc in next ch sp, hdc in next dc, ch 1, skip next pc], dc in next dc; repeat from * 2 more times; repeat between [ ], join with sl st in top of ch-3.
Rnd 4: Sl st in each of next 2 sts, sl st in next ch-3 sp, ch 3, (2 dc, ch 3, 3 dc) in same sp, *[ch 1, (3 dc in next ch-1 sp, ch 1) 2

times], (3 dc, ch 3, 3 dc) in next ch-3 sp; repeat from * 2 more times; repeat between [ ], join.
Rnd 5: Ch 1, sc in each st and in each ch-1 sp around with 5 dc in each corner ch-3 sp, join with sl st in first sc, fasten off (80 sc).
Holding Motifs wrong sides together, matching sts, with pink, sew together according to Assembly Diagram on page 104.

BORDER
Rnd 1: With D hook, join pink with sc in first st of any 5-sc group before one short end, sc in next st, *ch 2, skip next st, evenly space 145 sc across to center st of next 5-sc group*, ch 2, skip next st, evenly space 187 sc across to center st of next 5-sc group; repeat between **, ch 2, skip next st, evenly space 185 sc across, join with sl st in first sc (145 sc on each short edge between corner ch sps, 187 sc on each long edge between corner ch sps).
Rnd 2: Ch 3, *[skip next st, (pc, dc, ch 2, dc, pc) in next corner ch sp, skip next st, (dc in next st, pc in next st) across] to 2 sts before next corner ch sp, dc in next st; repeat from * 2 more times; repeat between [ ], join with sl st in top of ch-3, fasten off.

Diagram on page 104

New Baby on the Block

Traditional pastels and puffy clusters combine to create a classic blanket that will stand the test of time to become a treasured heirloom.

FIRST PANEL

Row 1: With white, ch 24, sc in 2nd ch from hook, sc in each ch across, turn (23 sc).

Rows 2-3: Ch 1, sc in each st across, turn.

Row 4: Ch 1, sc in each of first 3 sts, (sc in **front lp** of next st, sc in each of next 3 sts) across, turn.

Note: For **cluster (cl),** yo, insert hook in remaining lp of next st on row before last, yo, draw lp through, yo, draw through 2 lps on hook, (yo, insert hook in same st, yo, draw lp through, yo, draw through 2 lps on hook) 2 times, yo, draw through all 4 lps on hook, skip next st on last row.

Row 5: Ch 1, sc in each of first 3 sts, (cl, sc in each of next 3 sts) across, turn (18 sc, 5 cls).

Row 6: Ch 1, sc in first 5 sts, sc in **front lp** of next st, (sc in each of next 3 sts, sc in **front lp** of next st) 3 times, sc in last 5 sts, turn.

Row 7: Ch 1, sc in first 5 sts, cl, (sc in each of next 3 sts, cl) 3 times, sc in last 5 sts, turn (19 sc, 4 cls).

Rows 8-21: Repeat rows 4-7 consecutively, ending with row 5.

Rows 22-24: Ch 1, sc in each st across, turn. At end of last row, fasten off.

Row 25: Join blue with sc in first st, sc in each st across, turn.

Rows 26-48: Repeat rows 2-24.

Row 49: Join white with sc in first st, sc in each st across, turn.

Rows 50-168: Repeat rows 2-49 consecutively, ending with row 24.

For **right side edging,** with right side of work facing you, working in ends of rows across right edge, join white with sc in row 1, sc in same row, sc in each row across, fasten off (169 sc).

SECOND PANEL

Work same as First Panel, using pink as first color and white as 2nd color.

For **right side edging,** work same as First Panel's right side edging.

For **left side edging,** with right side of work facing you, working in ends of rows across left edge, join white with sc in row 168, sc in each row across to last row, 2 sc in last row, fasten off (169 sc).

THIRD PANEL

Work same as First Panel.

For **right side edging,** work same as First Panel's right side edging.

For **left side edging,** work same

Continued on page 104

Designed by
Roberta Maier

FINISHED SIZE
38" x 40".

MATERIALS
2-ply baby yarn — 14 oz. white; baby pompadour yarn — 5 oz. each pink and blue; 3 yds. blue ⅜" double-faced satin ribbon; four pink satin roses with leaves; white sewing thread; sewing needle; E crochet hook or size needed to obtain gauge.

GAUGE
5 sc = 1";
5 sc rows = 1".

SKILL LEVEL
Average

New Baby on the Block

Continued from page 103

as Second Panel's left side edging.

FOURTH PANEL

Work same as Second Panel.

FIFTH PANEL

Work same as Third Panel.

SIXTH PANEL

Work same as Second Panel.

SEVENTH PANEL

Work same as First Panel.

For **left side edging,** work same as Second Panel's left side edging.

To **join,** holding two Panels wrong sides together, matching sts and working through both thicknesses, join white with sl st in first st, (ch 1, sl st in next st) across, fasten off.

Join Panels together in the order in which they were worked.

TOP EDGING

Row 1: Working across top edge of Panels, join white with sc in first st, sc in each st and in end of each row across, turn (173 sc).

Row 2: For **beading row,** ch 3, dc in each of next 2 sts, ch 1, skip next st, (dc in next st, ch 1, skip next st) across to last 3 sts, dc in each of last 3 sts, turn.

Row 3: Ch 1, sc in each st and in each ch sp across, turn.

Rows 4-5: Ch 1, sc in each st across, turn.

Row 6: Ch 1, sc in first st, (sc in **front lp** of next st, sc in next st) across, turn.

Row 7: Ch 1, sc in first st, (cl, sc in next st) across, fasten off.

BOTTOM EDGING

Row 1: Working across bottom edge of Panels in starting ch on opposite side of row 1, join white with sc in first ch, sc in each ch and in end of each row across, turn (173 sc).

Rows 2-7: Repeat same rows of Top Edging.

BORDER

Rnd 1: Working around entire outer edge, join white with sc in any corner st, 2 sc in same st, sc in each st and in end of each row around with 3 sc in each corner st, join with sl st in first sc (173 sc on each short end between corner sts, 183 sc on each long edge between corner sts).

Rnds 2-4: Ch 1, sc in each st around with 3 sc in each center corner st, join.

Rnd 5: Ch 1, sc in first st, sc in **front lp** of next st, sc in next st, sc in **front lp** of next st, *[3 sc in next st, sc in **front lp** of next st, (sc in next st, sc in **front lp** of next st) across] to next corner st; repeat from * 2 more times; repeat between [ ], join.

Rnd 6: Ch 1, sc in first st, (cl, sc in next st) 2 times, *3 sc in next st, sc in next st, (cl, sc in next st) across to next corner st; repeat from * 2 more times, 3 sc in next st, (sc in next st, cl) across, join.

Rnd 7: Repeat rnd 2, fasten off.

FINISHING

Cut ribbon in half. Weave each piece through beading row on Top and Bottom Edgings, trim even with edges of Panels.

Sew one rose to each end of each beading row over ribbon.

Tender Innocence

Instructions on page 100

ASSEMBLY DIAGRAM

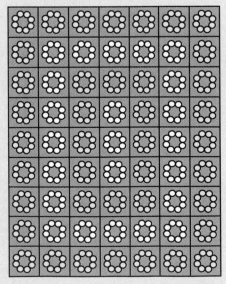

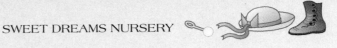

Quilted Pastels

Continued from page 99

Row 6: For **third triangle,** with yellow, repeat same row of second triangle.

Rows 7-13: Repeat same rows of first triangle.

Row 6: For **fourth triangle,** join blue with sc in same ch sp as last sc of first row on last triangle made, ch 1, skip next st, (sc in next st, ch 1, skip next st) 6 times, sc in same ch sp as first sc of first row on first triangle, turn.

Rows 7-13: Repeat same rows of first triangle.

Rnd 14: Working in ch sps and in ends of rows around outer edge, join white with sc in any corner ch sp, ch 3, sc in same sp, evenly space 10 sc across side of first triangle, hdc in next ch sp on rnd 5, *evenly space 10 sc across side of next triangle, (sc, ch 3, sc) in next corner ch sp, evenly space 10 sc across next side of same triangle, hdc in next ch sp on rnd 5; repeat from * 2 more times, evenly space 10 sc across other side of first triangle, join with sl st in first sc, fasten off (23 sc on each edge between corner ch sps).

Sew Blocks together in four rows of five Blocks each.

BORDER

Rnd 1: Working around entire outer edge, join white with sc in any corner ch sp, ch 3, sc in same sp, sc in each st, sc in each ch sp on each side of seams and hdc in each seam around with (sc, ch 3, sc) in each corner ch sp, join with sl st in first sc (103 sc on each short end between corner ch sps, 129 sc on each long edge between corner ch sps).

Rnd 2: Sl st in first ch sp, ch 1, (sc, ch 3, sc) in same sp, *[ch 1, skip next st, (sc in next st, ch 1, skip next st) across to next corner], (sc, ch 3, sc) in next corner ch sp; repeat from * 2 more times; repeat between [ ], join, fasten off.

Rnd 3: Join mint with sc in any corner ch sp, ch 3, sc in same sp, (sc, ch 2, sc) in each sc around with (sc, ch 3, sc) in each corner ch sp, join, **turn.**

Rnd 4: Sl st in next st, sl st in next ch sp, ch 3, *(hdc in next ch sp, ch 1) across to next corner ch sp, (hdc, ch 1, hdc, ch 3, hdc, ch 1, hdc) in next ch sp, ch 1; repeat from * around, join with sl st in 2nd ch of ch-3, **turn.**

Rnd 5: Sl st in first ch sp, ch 1, sc in same sp, ch 1, sc in next ch sp, ch 1, *[(sc, ch 3, sc) in next corner ch sp, ch 1, (sc in next ch sp, ch 1) across] to next corner ch sp; repeat from * 2 more times; repeat between [ ], join with sl st in first sc, **turn.**

Rnd 6: Sl st in first ch sp, ch 1, sc in same sp, *[ch 1, (sc in next ch sp, ch 1) across] to next corner ch sp, (sc, ch 3, sc) in next ch sp; repeat from * 3 more times; repeat between [ ], join, **turn,** fasten off.

Rnd 7: Join white with sc in top right-hand corner ch sp, ch 3, sc in same sp, sc in each st and in each ch-1 sp around with (sc, ch 3, sc) in each corner ch sp, join (119 sc on each short end between corner ch sps, 145 sc on each long edge between corner ch sps).

Note: For **small shell,** (2 dc, ch 2, 2 dc) in next st.

Rnd 8: Ch 1, sc in first st, *large shell in next ch sp, skip next 2 sts, sc in next st, skip next 2 sts, (small shell in next st, skip next 2 sts, sc in next st, skip next 2 sts) across to next corner ch sp, large shell in next ch sp*, sc in next st, (skip next 2 sts, small shell in next st, skip next 2 sts, sc in next st) across to next corner ch sp; repeat between **, (sc in next st, skip next 2 sts, small shell in next st, skip next 2 sts) across, join.

Rnd 9: Ch 1, sc in first st, ch 2, [skip next 2 sts, (sc, ch 3, sc) in next st, (sc, ch 4, sc) in next ch sp, (sc, ch 3, sc) in next st, ch 2, sc in next sc, ch 2, *(sc, ch 3, sc) in next small shell, ch 2, sc in next sc, ch 2; repeat from * across to next large shell]; repeat between [ ] 2 times, skip next 2 sts, (sc, ch 3, sc) in next st, (sc, ch 4, sc) in next ch sp, (sc, ch 3, sc) in next st, ch 2, ◊sc in next sc, ch 2, (sc, ch 3, sc) in next small shell, ch 2; repeat from ◊ across, join, fasten off.

Panda Parade

*Playful images and brilliant colors are perfect for sparking little
ones' minds and imaginations at naptime or at play.*

BLOCK (make 9)

Row 1: With pink, ch 40, sc in 2nd ch from hook, sc in each ch across, turn (39 sc).

Rows 2-4: Ch 1, sc in each st across, turn.

Notes: When changing colors *(see fig 11, page 159)*, always drop yarn to wrong side of work. Use a separate skein or ball of yarn for each color section. **Do not** carry yarn across from one section to another. Fasten off at end of each color section.

Work odd-numbered graph rows from right to left and even-numbered rows from left to right.

Each square on graph equals 1 sc.

Row 5: Ch 1, sc in first 11 sts changing to black in last st made, sc in next 7 sts changing to pink in last st made, sc in each of next 3 sts changing to black in last st made, sc in next 7 sts changing to pink in last st made, sc in each st across, turn.

Rows 6-53: Ch 1, sc in each st across changing colors according to graph, turn. At end of last row, **do not** turn.

Rnd 54: Working around outer edge, ch 1, sc in end of each row and in each st around with 3 sc in each corner, join with sl st in first sc, fasten off.

FINISHING

1: With white, using Satin Stitch (see illustration), embroider eyes centered over rows 41 and 42 of face 1½" apart. With black, using French Knot (see illustration), embroider pupil centered over each eye.

2: With black, using Satin Stitch, embroider nose over rows 36 and 38 centered below eyes.

3: With black, using Straight Stitch (see illustration), embroider mouth lines below nose over rows 34-36 as shown in photo.

4: Holding Blocks right sides together, matching sts, with pink, sew together through **back lps** in three rows of three Blocks each.

EDGING

Rnd 1: Working around entire outer edge in **back lps** only, join white with sc in any st, sc in each st and in each seam around with 3 sc in each corner, join with sl st in first sc, fasten off.

Rnd 2: Working this rnd in **back lps,** join black with sc in any st, sc in each st around with 3 sc in each center corner st, join, fasten off.

Graph on page 114

Designed by
Linda Everson

FINISHED SIZE
36" x 42".

MATERIALS
Worsted-weight yarn —
19 oz. pink, 9½ oz.
each white and black;
tapestry needle; G
crochet hook or size
needed to obtain gauge.

GAUGE
7 sc = 2"; 4 sc rows = 1".
Each Block is
11¾" x 13¾".

SKILL LEVEL
Average

SATIN STITCH

FRENCH KNOT

STRAIGHT STITCH

Heavenly Rainbows

Wrap your precious bundle in a little bit of heaven with this colorful afghan stitched in a textured pattern that will satisfy baby's need to touch.

PANEL (make 5)
Center Strip

Row 1: With white, ch 4, (dc, ch 3, 2 dc) in 4th ch from hook, turn (4 dc, 1 ch-3 sp).

Row 2: Ch 3, dc in next st, ch 2, (2 dc, ch 3, 2 dc) in next ch sp, ch 2, dc in each of last 2 sts, turn (8 dc, 3 ch sps).

Note: For **shell,** (2 dc, ch 2, 2 dc) in next ch sp.

Row 3: Ch 3, skip next st, shell in next ch sp, ch 8, skip next ch sp, shell in next ch sp, skip next st, dc in last st, turn (2 dc, 2 shells, 1 ch-8 lp).

Rows 4-78: Ch 3, shell in ch sp of next shell, ch 8, skip next ch-8 lp, shell in ch sp of next shell, dc in last st, turn.

Note: Working vertically across ch-8 lps to last row, insert hook in ch sp on row 2, draw through ch-8 lp on next row, pull up lp, (insert hook in lp just made, draw through ch-8 lp on next row) across. Secure last lp with bobby pin.

Row 79: Ch 3, shell in next shell, sc in next ch-8 lp, shell in next shell, dc in last st, turn.

Row 80: Sl st in each of first 3 sts, sl st in next ch sp, ch 2, yo, insert hook in same sp, yo, draw lp through, yo, draw through 2 lps on hook, yo, insert hook in next ch sp, yo, draw lp through, yo, draw through 2 lps on hook, yo, insert hook in same sp, yo, draw lp through, yo, draw through 2

lps on hook, yo, draw through all 4 lps on hook, fasten off.

Rnd 81: With right side of work facing you, working in ends of rows across left edge, join white with sl st in row 79, ch 3, (hdc, sc) in same row, 3 sc in next row, (2 sc in next row, 3 sc in next row) across to row 3, (sc, hdc, dc) in next row, ch 3, 3 dc in next row, ch 3; working on opposite side of row 1, (3 dc, ch 3, 3 dc) in sp between center 2 dc, ch 3, 3 dc in row 2, (dc, hdc, sc) in next row, 3 sc in next row, (2 sc in next row, 3 sc in next row) across to row 79, (sc, hdc, dc) in next row, ch 3, 3 dc in next shell on same row, ch 3, (3 dc, ch 3, 3 dc) around center of st on row 80, ch 3, 3 dc in next shell on row 79, ch 3, join with sl st in top of ch-3, fasten off.

Border

Notes: Work each sc in **back lp** only unless otherwise stated. Work each dc into unworked **front lps** on row before last; skip st on last row behind dc.

Do not turn at the end of each row. Leave a 7" end at the beginning and end of each row to be worked into Fringe.

Row 1: For **first side,** with right side of work facing you, skip first st on rnd 81 of Center Strip, join white with sc in next st, sc in next

Continued on page 115

Designed by
Sara Semonis

FINISHED SIZE
35" x 43"
not including Fringe.

MATERIALS
Sport yarn — 10½ oz.
white, 4 oz. each
peach, pink, lavender,
lt. blue, aqua, mint and
yellow; bobby pin;
tapestry needle; F
crochet hook or size
needed to obtain gauge.

GAUGE
9 sc = 2"; 4 sc
back lp rows = 1".

SKILL LEVEL
Average

Bubbles & Broomsticks

Sweep a favorite youngster off to dreamland covered from head to toe in a whimsical design featuring pretty lace and colorful scallops.

Designed by
Sandra Smith

FINISHED SIZE
35" x 38"
not including Fringe.

MATERIALS
Pompadour sport yarn
— 18 oz. white and
7 oz. variegated
pink/yellow/aqua;
No. 35 broomstick lace
pin; F crochet hook
or size needed to
obtain gauge.

GAUGE
3 5-loop broomstick
lace groups = 2½";
4 broomstick
lace rows = 3".

SKILL LEVEL
Average

FIRST PANEL

Row 1: With white, ch 15, **do not** turn; slip lp from hook onto broomstick pin *(see ill. No. 1 on page 115)*, insert hook in 2nd ch from pin, yo, draw lp through and slip onto pin, (insert hook in next ch, yo, draw lp through and slip onto pin) across, **do not** turn (15 lps on pin); [insert hook under first 5 lps on pin, slide lps off pin (see ill. No. 2), yo, draw lp through, ch 1, 5 sc in same 5-lp group (see ill. No. 3), *insert hook under next 5 lps on pin, slide off pin, yo, draw lp through, yo, draw through both lps on hook (first sc made), work 4 more sc in same 5-lp group; repeat from *], **do not** turn.

Rows 2-48: Slip last lp on hook onto pin, (insert hook in next st, yo, draw lp through st and slip onto pin) across; repeat between [ ] on row 1. At end of last row, fasten off.

Rnd 49: Working in sts and in ends of rows around outer edge, with right side of work facing you, join variegated with sl st in first ch on opposite side of starting ch on row 1, skip next 3 chs, 9 dc in next ch, skip next 2 chs, sl st in next ch, skip next 2 chs, 9 dc in next ch, skip next 3 chs, sl st in last ch; working in sc at ends of rows, 9 dc in first row, (sl st in next row, 9 dc in next row) across to last row, skip

last row, sl st in first st, skip next 3 sts, 9 dc in next st, skip next 2 sts, sl st in next st, skip next 2 sts, 9 dc in next st, skip next 3 sts, sl st in last st; working in sc at ends of rows, skip first row, 9 dc in next row, (sl st in next row, 9 dc in next row) across, join with sl st in first sl st, **turn,** fasten off.

Rnd 50: Working this rnd in **back lps** only, join white with sl st in first sl st on either short end, (sl st in next 9 dc, sl st in next sl st) 2 times, (sl st in next 5 dc, ch 1, sl st in next 4 dc, sl st in next sl st) 24 times, sl st in next 9 dc, (sl st in next sl st, sl st in next 9 dc) around, join with sl st in first sl st, fasten off.

SECOND PANEL

Rows/Rnd 1-49: Repeat same rows and rnd of First Panel.

Rnd 50: Working this rnd in **back lps** only, join white with sl st in first sl st on either short end, sl st in next 9 dc, sl st in next sl st, sl st in next 9 dc, (sl st in next sl st, sl st in next 5 dc, ch 1, sl st in next 4 dc) 24 times, (sl st in next sl st, sl st in next 9 dc) 2 times; to join Panels, holding wrong sides together, (sl st in next sl st, sl st in next 5 dc, ch 1, sl st in corresponding ch-1 sp on last Panel made, ch 1, sl st in next 4 dc on this Panel) 24 times, join with sl st in first sl st, fasten off.

Continued on page 115

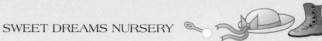

Party Gingham

Pretty pastels and clean, crisp white skip two-by-two across this thermal-style cover that will lend a festive mood to any nursery.

Designed by
Vicki M. Watkins

FINISHED SIZE
36" square
not including Fringe.

MATERIALS
3-ply sport yarn — 7 oz.
white, 2 oz. each lilac,
blue, pink, yellow
and green; G crochet
hook or size needed
to obtain gauge.

GAUGE
4 dc = 1";
2 dc rows = 1".

SKILL LEVEL
Average

AFGHAN

Notes: Each square on graph equals 2 dc.

Beginning ch-3 is used and counted as first st of each row.

When changing colors *(see fig. 11, page 159)*, always drop yarn to wrong side of work. Work over dropped color and pick up again when needed. Fasten off colors at end of each color section.

Work odd-numbered rows from right to left and even-numbered rows from left to right.

Row 1: With white, ch 146, dc in 4th ch from hook changing to yellow, dc in each of next 2 sts changing to white in last st made, (dc in each of next 2 sts changing to yellow in last st made, dc in each of next 2 sts changing to white in last st made) 5 times, (dc in each of next 2 sts changing to lavender in last st made, dc in each of next 2 sts changing to white in last st made) 6 times, (dc in each of next 2 sts changing to green in last st made, dc in each of next 2 sts changing to white in

last st made) 6 times, (dc in each of next 2 sts changing to pink in last st made, dc in each of next 2 sts changing to white in last st made) 6 times, (dc in each of next 2 sts changing to blue in last st made, dc in each of next 2 sts changing to white in last st made) 6 times, (dc in each of next 2 sts changing to yellow in last st made, dc in each of next 2 sts changing to white in last st made) 6 times, turn (144 dc).

Rows 2-72: Ch 3, dc in each st across changing colors according to graph, turn. At end of last row, fasten off.

FRINGE

For **each Fringe,** cut two strands white each 6" long. With both strands held together, fold in half, insert hook in st or row, draw fold through, draw all loose ends through fold, tighten. Trim ends.

Fringe in end of each row and in every other st around Afghan.

Graph on page 114

Party Gingham *Instructions on page 112*

COLOR CHANGE GRAPH

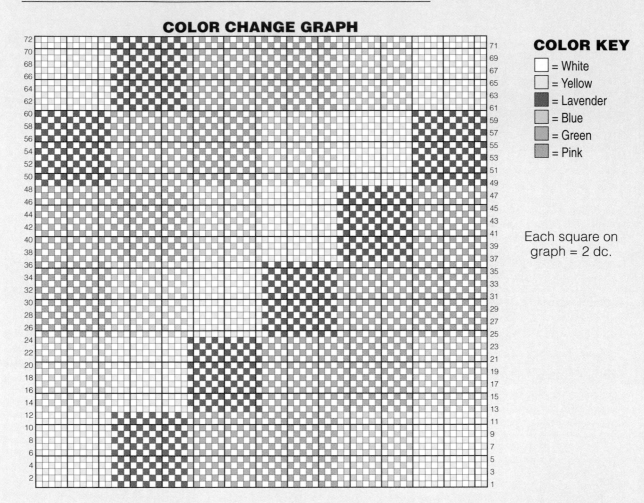

COLOR KEY

☐ = White
☐ = Yellow
■ = Lavender
☐ = Blue
☐ = Green
☐ = Pink

Each square on
graph = 2 dc.

Panda Parade *Continued from page 107*

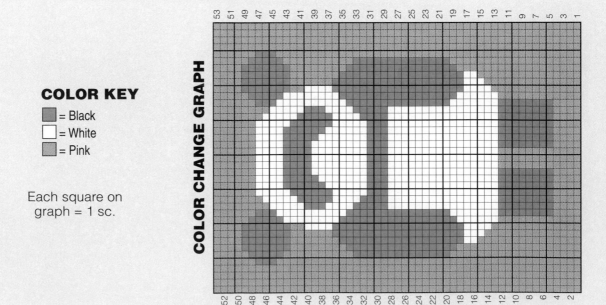

COLOR KEY

■ = Black
☐ = White
☐ = Pink

Each square on
graph = 1 sc.

Heavenly Rainbows

Continued from page 109

192 sts leaving remaining sts unworked, fasten off (193 sc).

Row 2: Join peach with sc in first st, sc in next 5 sts, dc in next st on row before last, (sc in next 11 sts, dc in next st on row before last, skip next st on last row) across to last 6 sts, sc in last 6 sts, fasten off.

Row 3: Join pink with sc in first st, sc in next 6 sts, dc in next st on row before last, sc in next 9 sts, (dc in next st on row before last, sc in next st, dc in next st on row before last, sc in next 9 sts) across to last 8 sts, dc in next st on row before last, sc in last 7 sts, fasten off.

Row 4: Join lavender with sc in first st, sc in next 7 sts, dc in next st on row before last, sc in next 7 sts, (dc in next st on row before last, sc in each of next 3 sts, dc in next st on row before last, sc in next 7 sts) across to last 9 sts, dc in next st on row before last, sc in last 8 sts, fasten off.

Row 5: Join lt. blue with sc in first st, sc in next 8 sts, dc in next st on row before last, (sc in next 5 sts, dc in next st on row before last) across to last 9 sts, sc in last 9 sts, fasten off.

Row 6: Join aqua with sc in first st, sc in next 9 sts, dc in next st on row before last, sc in each of next 3 sts, dc in next st on row before last, (sc in next 7 sts, dc in next st on row before last, sc in each of next 3 sts, dc in next st on row before last) across to last 10 sts, sc in last 10 sts, fasten off.

Row 7: Join mint with sc in first st, sc in next 10 sts, dc in next st on row before last, sc in next st, dc in next st on row before last, (sc in next 9 sts, dc in next st on row before last, sc in next st, dc in next st on row before last) across to last 11 sts, sc in last 11 sts, fasten off.

Row 8: Join yellow with sc in first st, sc in next 11 sts, dc in next st on row before last, (sc in next 11 sts, dc in next st on row before last) across to last 12 sts, sc in last 12 sts, fasten off.

Row 9: Working this row in **both lps,** join yellow with sc in first st, sc in each st across, fasten off.

Row 1: For **second side,** skipping next 13 sts on rnd 81 of Center Strip, repeat same row of first side.

Rows 2-9: Repeat same rows of first side. Matching sts, with yellow, sew last row of each Panel together through **back lps** only.

FRINGE

For **each Border Fringe,** cut one 14" strand to match color of row. Fold in half, insert hook in end of row, draw fold through, draw all loose ends through fold, tighten. Trim ends. Fringe each row on each end of Border.

For **each Center Strip Fringe,** using two 14" strands white, Fringe each ch sp on each end of Center Strip.

Bubbles & Broomsticks

Continued from page 110

Repeat Second Panel five more times for a total of seven Panels.

EIGHTH PANEL

Rows/Rnd 1-49: Repeat same rows and rnd of First Panel.

Rnd 50: Working this rnd in **back lps** only, join white with sl st in first sl st on either short end, sl st in next 9 dc, (sl st in next sl st, sl st in next 9 dc) 27 times, (sl st in next sl st, sl st in next 5 dc, ch 1, sl st in corresponding ch-1 sp on last Panel made, ch 1, sl st in next 4 dc on this Panel) 24 times, join with sl st in first sl st, fasten off.

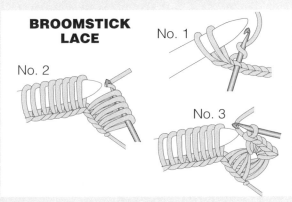

BROOMSTICK LACE

No. 1

No. 2

No. 3

THE MON

The Social Kit

WELCOME TO OUR PARTY

Family
Gatherings

Homespun Harmony

Comfortable colors, fitly blended in cheerful stripes, make this afghan one your family will reach for time and time again.

AFGHAN

Row 1: With off-white, ch 113, hdc in 3rd ch from hook, hdc in each ch across, turn (112 hdc).

Note: For **cross stitch (cr st),** skip next st, dc in next st; working over last st made, dc in skipped st.

Row 2: Ch 2, cr st across to last st, hdc in last st, turn (55 cr sts, 2 hdc).

Row 3: Ch 2, hdc in each st across, turn, fasten off.

Row 4: Join lt. green with sl st in first st, ch 2, *(tr, sc) in next st, skip next st; repeat from * across to last st, hdc in last st, turn, fasten off.

Row 5: Join orange with sl st in first st, ch 2, hdc in each st across, turn, fasten off.

Row 6: Repeat row 4.

Row 7: Join off-white with sl st in first st, ch 2, hdc in each st across, turn.

Row 8: Ch 2, cr st across to last st, hdc in last st, turn.

Row 9: Ch 2, hdc in each st across, turn, fasten off.

Row 10: With rose, repeat row 4.

Row 11: With yellow, repeat row 5.

Row 12: With rose, repeat row 4.

Rows 13-15: Repeat rows 7-9.

Row 16: With lavender, repeat row 4.

Row 17: With pink, repeat row 5.

Row 18: With lavender, repeat row 4.

Rows 19-21: Repeat rows 7-9.

Row 22: With peach, repeat row 4.

Row 23: With lt. green, repeat row 5.

Row 24: With peach, repeat row 4.

Rows 25-27: Repeat rows 7-9.

Row 28: With yellow, repeat row 4.

Row 29: With rose, repeat row 5.

Row 30: With yellow, repeat row 4.

Rows 31-33: Repeat rows 7-9.

Row 34: With pink, repeat row 4.

Row 35: With lavender, repeat row 5.

Row 36: With pink, repeat row 4.

Rows 37-39: Repeat rows 7-9.

Rows 40-129: Repeat rows 4-39 consecutively, ending with row 21.

Rnd 130: Working in sts and in ends of rows around outer edge, join variegated with sc in first st, 2 sc in same st, sc in each st across to last st, 3 sc in last st; evenly space 4 sc across every 3 rows across; working in starting ch on

Continued on page 134

Designed by
Lena Chamberlain

FINISHED SIZE
38½" x 57½"
not including Fringe.

MATERIALS
Worsted-weight yarn —
24 oz. off-white, 5 oz.
each peach, yellow,
rose, lt. green, lavender,
pink and variegated;
1 crochet hook or size
needed to obtain gauge.

GAUGE
3 hdc = 1";
Rows 1-12 = 5½".

SKILL LEVEL
Average

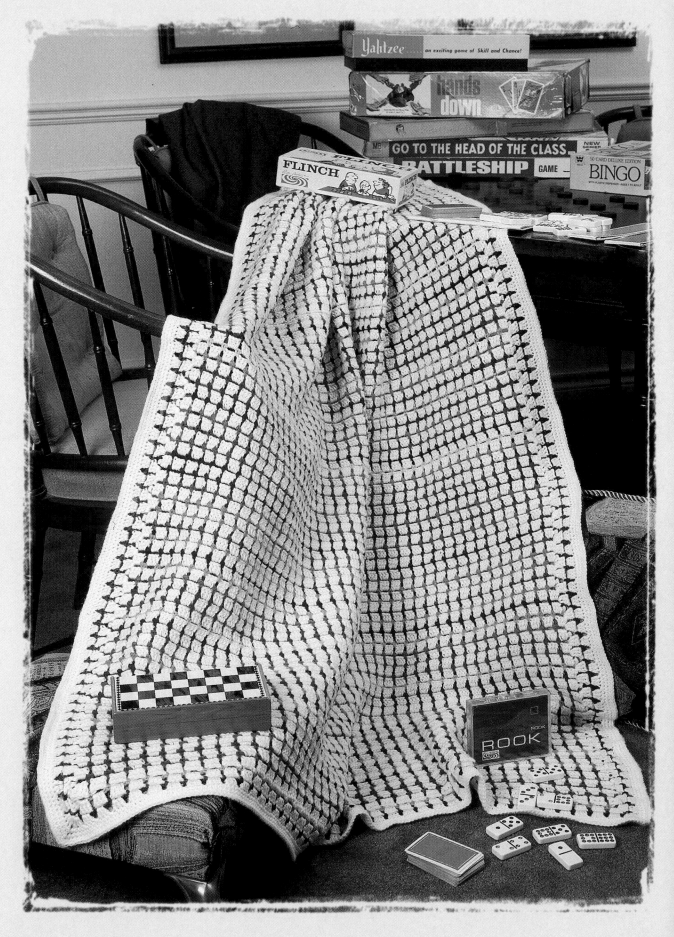

Touched by Color

Grab your favorite board games and head for the floor, accompanied by this ample cover checkered with bright shades of scrap yarn.

AFGHAN

Row 1: With off-white, ch 202, dc in 4th ch from hook, dc in each of next 2 chs, (ch 1, skip next ch, dc in each of next 3 chs) across, **do not** turn, drop off-white (151 dc, 49 ch-1 sps).

Row 2: Join any color scrap yarn with sc in first st, ch 3, skip next 3 sts, (sc in next ch-1 sp, ch 3, skip next 3 sts) across, sl st in dropped lp on last row, turn, fasten off (50 sc, 50 ch-3 sps).

Row 3: Pick up off-white, sl st in first sl st, ch 3, 3 dc in next ch-3 sp, (ch 1, 3 dc in next ch-3 sp) across, **do not** turn, drop off-white.

Rows 4-200: Repeat rows 2 and 3 alternately, ending with row 2. At end of last row, fasten off off-white.

Row 201: Working in starting ch on opposite side of row 1, join any color scrap yarn with sc in first ch, ch 3, skip next 2 chs, sc in next ch-1 sp, (ch 3, skip next 3 chs, sc in next ch-1 sp) across to last 4 chs, ch 3, skip next 3 chs, sc in last ch, turn, fasten off.

BORDER

Notes: For **beginning shell (beg shell),** ch 3, (2 dc, ch 2, 3 dc) in same sp.

For **shell,** (3 dc, ch 2, 3 dc) in next ch sp.

Rnd 1: Working around outer edge in sts and in ends of rows, join off-white with sl st in top right corner ch-3 sp, beg shell, *ch 1, (3 dc in next ch-3 sp, ch 1) across to last ch-3 sp, shell in next corner, ch 1, skip next dc row, (3 dc in next sc row, ch 1) across* to last sc row, shell in next corner; repeat between **, join with sl st in top of ch-3, fasten off.

Rnd 2: Join any color scrap yarn with sc in any ch-2 sp, ch 2, sc in same sp, *[ch 3, (sc in next ch-1 sp, ch 3) across] to next corner ch-2 sp, (sc, ch 2, sc) in next ch sp; repeat from * 2 more times; repeat between [ ], join with sl st in first sc, fasten off.

Rnd 3: Join off-white with sl st in any corner ch-2 sp, beg shell, *[ch 1, (3 dc in next ch-3 sp, ch 1) across] to next corner ch-2 sp, shell in next ch-2 sp; repeat from * 2 more times; repeat between [ ], join with sl st in top of ch-3.

Rnd 4: Ch 1, sc in each st and in each ch-1 sp around with 3 sc in each corner ch-2 sp, join with sl st in first sc.

Rnds 5-6: Ch 1, sc in each st around with 3 sc in each center corner st, join. At end of last rnd, fasten off.

Designed by
Darla J. Fanton

FINISHED SIZE
45" x 76".

MATERIALS
Worsted-weight yarn — 43 oz. off-white and 15 oz. scrap yarn in assorted colors; G crochet hook or size needed to obtain gauge.

SPECIAL NOTES
Each row that calls for scrap yarn uses approximately 8 yds. of yarn. Each rnd on Border that calls for scrap yarn uses approximately 38 yds. of yarn.

GAUGE
4 3-dc groups and 3 ch-1 sps = 3"; 5 dc rows and 5 sc rows = 3½".

SKILL LEVEL
Average

Cranberry Frost

At journey's end, friends and loved ones will rest easy under this pleasant pairing of light and dark shades of burgundy.

Designed by
Lisa Thomm

FINISHED SIZE
45" x 63".

MATERIALS
Worsted-weight yarn —
43 oz. each claret and
lt. berry; N crochet
hook or size needed
to obtain gauge.

GAUGE
With 2 strands held
together, 3 sc and 3
shells = 7"; 7 sc rows
and 7 shell rows = 9".

SKILL LEVEL
Average

AFGHAN

Notes: Use one strand of each color held together throughout.

For **shell,** (dc, ch 1, dc, ch 1, dc) in next ch or st.

For **popcorn (pc),** 4 dc in next st, drop lp from hook, insert hook in first st of 4-dc group, pick up dropped lp, draw through st, ch 1. Push to right side of work.

Row 1: Ch 138, sc in 2nd ch from hook, (ch 1, skip next 3 chs, shell in next ch, ch 1, skip next 3 chs, sc in next ch) across, turn (18 sc, 17 shells). Front of row 1 is right side of work.

Row 2: Ch 6, sc in center dc of next shell, ch 3, (pc in next sc, ch 3, sc in center dc of next shell, ch 3) across to last st, dc in last st, turn.

Row 3: Ch 1, sc in first st, ch 1, shell in next sc, ch 1, (sc in next pc, ch 1, shell in next sc, ch 1) across to ch-6, sc in 3rd ch of ch-6, turn.

Rows 4-91: Repeat rows 2 and 3 alternately.

Rnd 92: Working around outer edge in sts and in ends of rows, ch 1, 3 sc in first st; skipping each ch-1 sp, sc in each st across with 3 sc in last st; *skip first row, (2 sc in next row, sc in next row) across*; working in starting ch on opposite side of row 1, 3 sc in first ch, sc in next ch sp, (sc in next ch, sc in next ch sp) across to last ch, 3 sc in last ch; repeat between **, join with sl st in first sc, **turn** (67 sc on each short end between corner 3-sc groups, 135 sc on each long edge between corner 3-sc groups).

Rnd 93: Ch 1, sc in first st, *[ch 5, skip next st, (sc in next st, ch 5, skip next st) across to 3 sc at next corner], (ch 5, sc in next sc) 3 times; repeat from * 2 more times; repeat between [ ], ch 5, (sc in next sc, ch 5) 2 times, join.

Rnd 94: Sl st in each of first 2 chs, ch 1, sc in same ch sp, ch 5, *[(sc in next ch sp, ch 5) across to 2 ch sps at next corner, (sc, ch 5, sc, ch 5, sc, ch 5) in each of next 2 ch sps; repeat from * around, join.

Rnd 95: Sl st in each of first 2 chs, ch 1, sc in same ch sp, ch 5, *(sc in next ch sp, ch 5) across to 3 ch sps at next corner, (sc, ch 5, sc, ch 5, sc, ch 5) in each of next 3 ch sps; repeat from * 3 more times, sc in last ch sp, ch 5, join, fasten off.

Jewels of Time

Like the laughter of a friend or the smiles of a child, this attractive cover in a unique shell pattern will warm your heart for years to come.

AFGHAN

Row 1: With teal, ch 188, sc in 2nd ch from hook, sc in each ch across, turn (187 sc).

Notes: For **shell**, (3 dc, ch 1, 3 dc) in next st.

For **long double crochet (ldc),** working over previous sts, yo, insert hook in st indicated, yo, draw up long lp, complete as dc.

Row 2: Ch 1, sc in first st, (skip next 2 sts, shell in next st, skip next 2 sts, sc in next st) across, turn (32 sc, 31 shells).

Row 3: Ch 3, dc in same st, skip next 3 sts, sc in next ch sp, (skip next 3 dc and next sc, 3 dc in next dc, ch 1; working over last 3 dc, 3 ldc in 3rd skipped dc, sc in next ch sp) across to last 4 sts, skip next 3 sts, 2 dc in last st, turn.

Row 4: Ch 1, sc in first st, skip next dc and next sc, 3 dc in next dc, ch 1; working over last 3 dc, 3 ldc in skipped dc, (sc in next ch-1 sp, skip next 3 dc and next sc, 3 dc in next dc, ch 1; working over last 3 dc, 3 ldc in 3rd skipped dc) across to last st, sc in last st, turn.

Rows 5-11: Repeat rows 3 and 4 alternately, ending with row 3. At end of last row, fasten off.

Row 12: Join beige with sc in first st, skip next dc and next sc, 3 dc in next dc, ch 1; working over last 3 dc, 3 ldc in skipped dc, (sc

in next ch-1 sp, skip next 3 dc and next sc, 3 dc in next dc, ch 1; working over last 3 dc, 3 dc in 3rd skipped dc) across to last st, sc in last st, turn.

Row 13: Repeat row 3, fasten off.

Row 14: With burgundy, repeat row 12.

Rows 15-24: Repeat rows 3 and 4 alternately. At end of last row, fasten off.

Row 25: Join beige with sl st in first st, ch 3, dc in same st, skip next 3 sts, sc in next ch sp, (skip next 3 dc and next sc, 3 dc in next dc, ch 1; working over last 3 dc, 3 ldc in 3rd skipped dc, sc in next ch sp) across to last 4 sts, skip next 3 sts, 2 dc in last st, turn.

Row 26: Repeat row 4, fasten off.

Row 27: With teal, repeat row 25.

Row 28: Repeat row 4.

Rows 29-37: Repeat rows 3 and 4 alternately, ending with row 3.

Rows 38-89: Repeat rows 12-37 consecutively. At end of last row, **do not** turn.

Row 90: Working in ends of rows, *(skip next row, 3 dc in next row, ch 1; working over last 3 dc, 3 ldc in skipped row, skip next row, sc in next row) 4 times, (skip next row, 3 dc in next row,

Continued on page 134

Designed by
Daisy Watson

FINISHED SIZE
65" x 67½"

MATERIALS
Worsted-weight yarn —
45½ oz. teal, 29 oz.
burgundy and 14½ oz.
beige; K crochet hook
or size needed to
obtain gauge.

GAUGE
1 sc and 1 shell = 2";
8 pattern rows = 6".

SKILL LEVEL
Average

Southwest Echoes

Visions of sunset in a painted desert will fill your den or living area decorated with this decidedly masculine Indian-style blanket.

Designed by
Francine Marlin

FINISHED SIZE
44½" x 72".

MATERIALS
Sport yarn — 787 yds. each purple and green, 590 yds. each orange and lt. rust, 394 yds. each pink, gold and burgundy; Mohair sport yarn — 787 yds. each purple and green, 590 yds. each orange and lt. rust, 394 yds. each pink, gold and burgundy; I crochet hook or size needed to obtain gauge.

GAUGE
With 2 strands held together, 3 sc = 1"; 7 sc rows = 2".

SKILL LEVEL
Advanced

AFGHAN
Notes: Use one strand each sport and mohair of same color held together throughout. (If desired, substitute one strand fuzzy chunky yarn for two strands sport yarn.)

When changing colors *(see fig. 11, page 159)*, always drop last color used to wrong side of work. **Do not** carry dropped color across to next section of same color. Use a separate ball of yarn for each color section. Fasten off at the end of each color section.

Graph is worked from right to left for odd rows and from left to right for even rows.

Each square on graph equals one sc.

Row 1: With gold, ch 134, sc in 2nd ch from hook, sc in each ch across, turn (133 sc).

Rows 2-8: Ch 1, sc in each st across, turn. At end of last row, fasten off.

Rows 9-28: Ch 1, sc in each st across changing colors according to Graph A on page 128, turn.

Rows 29-38: Ch 1, sc in each st across, turn. At end of last row, fasten off.

Row 39: Join lt. rust with sc in first st, sc in each st across, turn.

Rows 40-42: Ch 1, sc in each st across, turn.

Rows 43-62: Ch 1, sc in each st across changing colors according to Graph B, turn.

Rows 63-66: Ch 1, sc in each st across, turn. At end of last row, fasten off.

Row 67: Join gold with sc in first st, sc in each st across, turn.

Rows 68-70: Ch 1, sc in each st across, turn. At end of last row, fasten off.

Row 71: Join green with sc in first st, sc in each st across, turn.

Rows 72-74: Ch 1, sc in each st across, turn.

Rows 75-98: Ch 1, sc in each st across changing colors according to Graph C, turn.

Rows 99-102: Ch 1, sc in each st across, turn. At end of last row, fasten off.

Row 103: Join orange with sc in first st, sc in each st across, turn.

Rows 104-106: Ch 1, sc in each st across, turn. At end of last row, fasten off.

Rows 107-118: Working in color sequence of purple, pink and burgundy, repeat rows 103-106 consecutively.

Row 119: Join lt. rust with sc in first st, sc in each st across, turn.

Rows 120-134: Ch 1, sc in each st across, turn. At end of last row, fasten off.

Rows 135-150: Working in

Continued on page 128

Southwest Echoes

Continued from page 126

color sequence of burgundy, pink, purple and orange, repeat rows 103-106 consecutively.

Rows 151-154: Repeat rows 71-74.

Rows 155-178: Ch 1, sc in each st across changing colors according to Graph D, turn.

Rows 179-182: Ch 1, sc in each st across, turn. At end of last row, fasten off.

Rows 183-186: With gold, repeat rows 103-106.

Rows 187-214: Repeat rows 39-66.

Row 215: Join purple with sc in first st, sc in each st across, turn.

Rows 216-224: Ch 1, sc in each st across, turn.

Rows 225-244: Ch 1, sc in each st across changing colors according to Graph E, turn. At end of last row, fasten off.

Row 245: Join gold with sc in first st, sc in each st across, turn.

Rows 246-252: Ch 1, sc in each st across, turn. At end of last row, fasten off.

COLOR KEY

■ = Purple
■ = Burgundy
■ = Lt. Rust
■ = Orange
■ = Green
■ = Pink

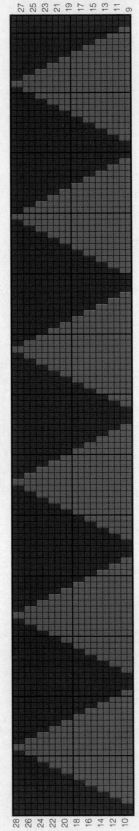

SOUTHWEST GRAPH A

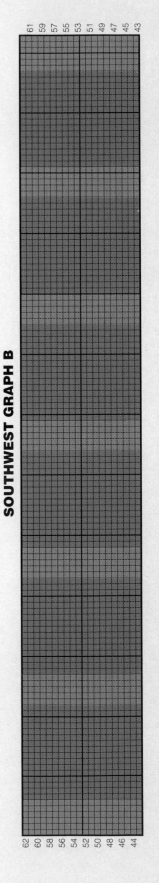

SOUTHWEST GRAPH B

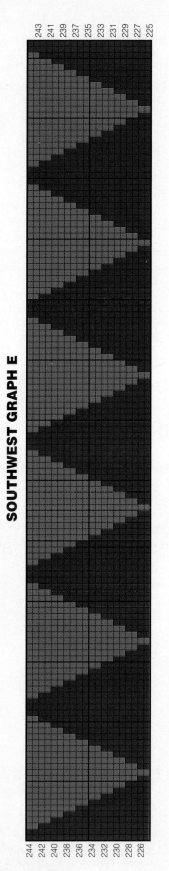

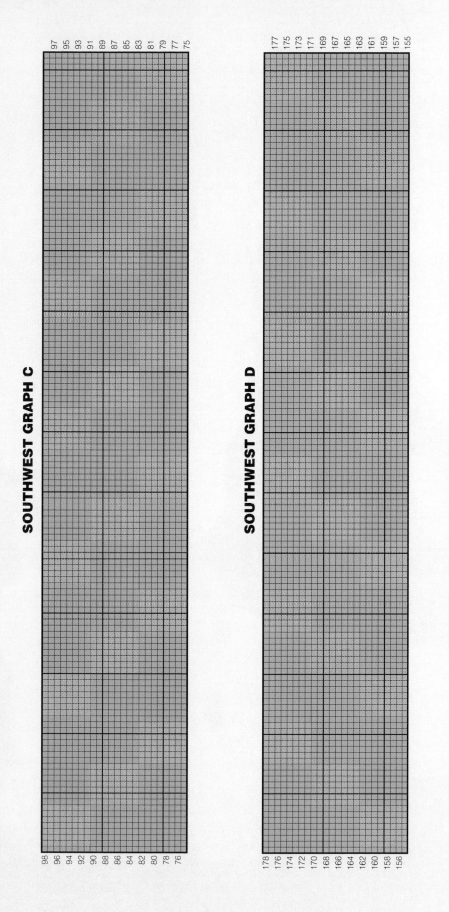

SOUTHWEST GRAPH C

97 95 93 91 89 87 85 83 81 79 77 75

98 96 94 92 90 88 86 84 82 80 78 76

SOUTHWEST GRAPH D

177 175 173 171 169 167 165 163 161 159 157 155

178 176 174 172 170 168 166 164 162 160 158 156

SOUTHWEST GRAPH E

243 241 239 237 235 233 231 229 227 225

244 242 240 238 236 234 232 230 228 226

Portrait of Santa

Christmas will be an extra-special time with a jolly, larger-than-life St. Nick to help add homey charm to the atmosphere.

AFGHAN

Row 1: With green, ch 180, sc in 2nd ch from hook, sc in each ch across, turn (179 sc).

Rows 2-259: Ch 1, sc in each st across, turn. At end of last row, fasten off.

SANTA

Hat

Row 1: Starting at tip of Hat, with red, ch 2, (sc, hdc) in 2nd ch from hook, turn (2 sts).

Row 2: Ch 3, hdc in 3rd ch from hook, (sc, hdc) in each of last 2 sts, turn (6).

Row 3: Ch 3, sc in 2nd ch from hook, hdc in next ch, (sc in next st, hdc in next st) across, turn (8).

Row 4: Ch 1, sc in first st, (hdc in next st, sc in next st) across to last st, (hdc, sc) in last st, turn (9).

Row 5: Ch 4, hdc in 3rd ch from hook, sc in next ch, (hdc in next st, sc in next st) across to last st, (hdc, sc) in last st, turn (13).

Row 6: Ch 2, (sc in next st, hdc in next st) across, turn.

Row 7: Ch 3, hdc in 3rd ch from hook, (sc in next st, hdc in next st) across to last st, (sc, hdc) in last st, turn (16).

Row 8: Ch 1, sc in first st, hdc in next st, (sc in next st, hdc in next st) across, turn.

Row 9: Ch 17, sc in 2nd ch from hook, (hdc in next ch or st, sc in next ch or st) across to last st, (hdc, sc) in last st, turn (33).

Row 10: Ch 2, hdc in same st, (sc in next st, hdc in next st) across, turn (34).

Row 11: Ch 4, sc in 3rd ch from hook, hdc in next ch, (sc in next st, hdc in next st) across, turn (37).

Row 12: Ch 1, sc in first st, hdc in next st, (sc in next st, hdc in next st) across to last st, (sc, hdc) in last st, turn (38).

Row 13: Ch 3, hdc in 3rd ch from hook, (sc in next st, hdc in next st) across, turn (40).

Row 14: Repeat row 8.

Row 15: Ch 5, hdc in 3rd ch from hook, sc in next ch, hdc in next ch, sc in next st, (hdc in next st, sc in next st) across to last st, (hdc, sc) in last st, turn (45).

Row 16: Repeat row 10 (46).

Row 17: Repeat row 8.

Row 18: Ch 1, sc in first st, (hdc in next st, sc in next st) across to last st, (hdc, sc) in last st, turn (47).

Row 19: Ch 2, hdc in same st, sc in next st, (hdc in next st, sc in next st) across to last st, (hdc, sc) in last st, turn (49).

Row 20: Repeat row 10 (50).

Row 21: Repeat row 13 (52).

Row 22: Ch 3, hdc in 3rd ch from hook, sc in next st, (hdc in

Continued on page 134

Designed by Francine Marlin

FINISHED SIZE
36" x 47".

MATERIALS
Worsted-weight yarn — 66½ oz. green, 8 oz. white, 4 oz. red, 2 oz. beige, small amount each rose and black; worsted-weight mohair yarn — 6½ oz. white; tapestry needle; E crochet hook or size needed to obtain gauge.

GAUGE
5 sc = 1"; 11 sc rows = 2".

SKILL LEVEL
Average

Treble-Toned Shells

Chunky shells in bright, patriotic tones lend lively appeal to that comfy old chair or inviting ease to a family room sofa.

Designed by
Maggie Weldon
*for Monsanto's
Designs for America
Program*

FINISHED SIZE
45" x 65".

MATERIALS
Worsted-weight yarn —
38 oz. each dk. rose
and blue, 29½ oz.
off-white; Q hook or
size needed to
obtain gauge.

GAUGE
With 3 strands held
together, 2 shells = 7";
1 shell row = 2".

SKILL LEVEL
Easy

AFGHAN

Notes: Use 3 strands of same color held together throughout.

Do not turn at the end of each row.

For **shell,** 5 dc in next st or ch.

Row 1: With blue, ch 59, shell in 6th ch from hook, (skip next 4 chs, shell in next ch) across to last 3 chs, skip next 2 chs, dc in last ch, **do not** turn, fasten off (11 shells, 2 dc).

Row 2: Join off white with sl st in first st, ch 3, 2 dc in same st; (working in front of last row, skip next shell, shell in 2nd skipped ch on starting ch) 10 times, 3 dc in last st on last row, fasten off (10 shells, 6 dc).

Row 3: Join dk. rose with sl st in first st, ch 3; (working in front of last row, shell in 3rd dc of next shell on row before last) 11 times, dc in last st on last row, fasten off.

Row 4: Join blue with sl st in first st, ch 3, 2 dc in same st; (working in front of last row, skip next shell, shell in center dc of next shell on row before last) 10 times, 3 dc in last st on last row, fasten off.

Row 5: With off-white, repeat row 3.

Row 6: With dk. rose, repeat row 4.

Row 7: With blue, repeat row 3.

Row 8: With off-white, repeat row 4.

Rows 9-67: Repeat rows 3-8 consecutively, ending with row 7.

BORDER

Working in sts and in ends of rows, join dk. rose with sl st in first st on last row, ch 3, (dc, ch 2, 2 dc) in same st, dc in each of next 2 sts, skip next st, dc in each of next 2 sts; (working in front of last row, tr in center dc of next shell on row before last, dc in each of next 2 sts on last row, skip next row, dc in each of next 2 sts) across to last st, (2 dc, ch 2, 2 dc) in last st, dc in each row across; working in starting ch on opposite side of row 1, (2 dc, ch 2, 2 dc) in first ch, dc in each ch across to last ch, (2 dc, ch 2, 2 dc) in last ch, dc in each row across, join with sl st in top of ch-3, fasten off.

Homespun Harmony

Continued from page 119

opposite side of row 1, 3 sc in first ch, sc in each ch across to last ch, 3 sc in last ch; evenly space 4 sc across every 3 rows across, join with sl st in first sc, **turn.**

Rnd 131: Ch 1, (hdc, sc) in first st, *[(hdc, sc) in next st, skip next st*; repeat between ** across to 3 sc at next corner, (hdc, sc) in each of next 3 sts]; repeat between [ ] 2 more times; repeat between ** across to last 2 sts, (hdc, sc) in each of last 2 sts, join, fasten off.

FRINGE

For **each Fringe,** cut two strands variegated each 8" long. With both strands held together, fold in half; insert hook in st, draw fold through st, draw all loose ends through fold, tighten. Trim ends.

Fringe in each st on short ends of Afghan.

Jewels of Time

Continued from page 125

ch 1; working over last 3 dc, 3 ldc in skipped row, sc in next row) 2 times*; repeat between ** across to last row, skip last row; working in starting ch on opposite side of row 1, sc in first ch, (skip next 2 chs, 3 dc in next ch, ch 1; working over last 3 dc, 3 ldc in 2nd skipped ch, skip next ch, sc in next ch) across; repeat between ** across ends of rows, join with sl st in first st on row 89, fasten off.

Portrait of Santa

Continued from page 131

next st, sc in next st) across to last st, (hdc, sc) in last st, turn (55).

Row 23: Repeat row 10 (56).

Row 24: Repeat row 8.

Row 25: Ch 9, sc in 2nd ch from hook, hdc in next ch, (sc in next ch, hdc in next ch) 3 times, (sc in next st, hdc in next st) across, turn (64).

Row 26: Ch 3, sc in 2nd ch from hook, hdc in next ch, sc in next st, (hdc in next st, sc in next st) across to last st, (hdc, sc) in last st, turn (67).

Row 27: Ch 6, sc in 2nd ch from hook, (hdc in next ch, sc in next ch) 2 times, (hdc in next st, sc in next st) across to last st, (hdc, sc) in last st, turn (73).

Row 28: Ch 2, hdc in same st, sc in next st, (hdc in next st, sc in next st) across to last st, (hdc, sc) in last st, turn (75).

Row 29: Repeat row 10 (76).

Row 30: Ch 2, (hdc, sc) in same st, hdc in next, st, (sc in next st, hdc in next st) across, turn (78).

Row 31: Repeat row 8.

Row 32: Repeat row 4 (79).

Row 33: Ch 2, hdc in same st, sc in next st, (hdc in next st, sc in next st) across to last st, (hdc, sc) in last st, turn (81).

Row 34: Repeat row 10 (82).

Row 35: Repeat row 8.

Row 36: Repeat row 4 (83).

Row 37: Repeat row 10 (84).

Row 38: Repeat row 8.

Row 39: Repeat row 4 (85).

Row 40: Repeat row 19 (87).

Row 41: Ch 2, (sc in next st, hdc in next st) across, turn.

Row 42: Ch 1, sc in first st, hdc in next st, (sc in next st, hdc in next st) across to last st, (sc, hdc) in last st, turn (88).

Row 43: Repeat row 8.

Row 44: For **first side,** ch 1, sc in first st, (hdc in next st, sc in next st) 7 times, sc in next st, sl st in each of next 2 sts leaving remaining sts unworked, turn (16).

Row 45: Skip first sl st, sl st in next sl st, (sc in next st, hdc in next st) across, turn.

Row 46: Ch 1, sc in first st, (hdc in next st, sc in next st) 2 times, sc in next st, sl st in each of next 2 sts leaving remaining sts unworked, turn (8).

Row 47: Skip first sl st, sl st in next st, (sc in next st, hdc in next st) across, turn, fasten off.

Row 44: For **second side,** skip next 36 sts on row 43, join red with sc in next st, hdc in next st, (sc in next st, hdc in next st) across, turn (34).

Row 45: Ch 1, sc in first st, (hdc in next st, sc in next st) across to last 3 sts, sc in next st, sl st in each of last 2 sts, turn.

Row 46: Skip first sl st, sl st in next sl st, (sc in next st, hdc in next st) across, turn (32).

Row 47: Ch 1, sc in first st, (hdc in next st, sc in next st) 12 times, sc in next st, sl st in each of next 2 sts leaving remaining sts unworked, turn.

Row 48: Skip first sl st, sl st in next sl st, sc in next st, (hdc in next st, sc in next st) across to last st, (hdc, sc) in last st, turn (27).

Row 49: Ch 2, hdc in same st, (sc in next st, hdc in next st) 11 times, sc in next st, sl st in each of next 2 sts leaving remaining sts unworked, turn.

Row 50: Ch 1, skip first sl st, sl st in next st, sc in next st, (sc in next st, hdc in next st) across, turn (25).

Row 51: Ch 1, sc in first st, (hdc in next st, sc in next st) 10 times, sc in next st, sl st in each of next 2 sts leaving last st unworked, turn.

Row 52: Repeat row 45 (22).

Row 53: Ch 1, sc in first st, (hdc in next st, sc in next st) 9 times, sc in next st, sl st in each of next 2 sts, turn.

Row 54: Repeat row 45 (20).

Row 55: Ch 1, sc in first st, (hdc in next st, sc in next st) 7 times, sc in next st, sl st in each of next 2 sts leaving remaining sts unworked, turn.

Row 56: Repeat row 45 (16).

Row 57: Ch 1, sc in first st, (hdc in next st, sc in next st) 5 times, sc in next st, sl st in each of next 2 sts leaving remaining sts unworked, turn.

Row 58: Repeat row 45 (12).

Row 59: Ch 1, sc in first st, (hdc in next st, sc in next st) 4 times, sc in next st, sl st in each of next 2 sts, turn.

Row 60: Ch 1, skip first sl st, sl st in next st, (sc in next st, hdc in next st) across to last 2 sts, sc last 2 sts tog, turn (9).

Row 61: Ch 2, hdc in same st, sc in next st, hdc in next st, sc in each of next 2 sts, sl st in next st leaving remaining sts unworked, turn.

Row 62: Ch 1, skip first sl st, sl st in next st, sc in each of next 2 sts, hdc in next st, sc in next st leaving last ch-2 unworked, fasten off.

Hat Brim

Row 1: With white mohair, ch 95, sc in 2nd ch from hook, sc in each ch across, turn (94 sc).

Rows 2-9: Ch 1, sc in each st across, turn. At end of last row, fasten off.

Pom-Pom

Rnd 1: With white, ch 2, 6 sc in 2nd ch from hook, join with sl st in first sc (6 sc).

Rnd 2: Ch 1, 2 sc in each st around, join (12).

Rnd 3: Ch 1, sc in first st, 2 sc in next st, (sc in next st, 2 sc in next st) around, join (18).

Rnd 4: Ch 1, sc in each of first 2 sts, 2 sc in next st, (sc in each of next 2 sts, 2 sc in next st) around, join, fasten off (24).

Holly Leaf (make 2)

With green, ch 12, sc in 2nd ch from hook, *hdc in next ch, (dc in next ch, tr in next ch, dc in next ch, hdc in next ch) 2 times, sc in last ch, ch 2*; working on opposite side of starting ch, sc in next ch; repeat between **, join with sl st in first sc,

Continued on page 136

Portrait of Santa

Continued from page 135

fasten off.

For **berry,** join red with sl st in tip of one Leaf, ch 3, 4 dc in same sp, drop lp from hook, insert hook in top of ch-3, pick up dropped lp, draw through st, ch 1, fasten off.

Repeat on other Leaf.

Mustache

Row 1: With white, ch 20, sc in 2nd ch from hook, sc in each ch across, turn (19 sc).

Row 2: Ch 1, 2 sc in first st, sc in each st across to last 2 sts, sc last 2 sts tog, turn.

Row 3: Ch 1, sc first 2 sts tog, sc in each st across to last st, 2 sc in last st, turn.

Row 4: Repeat row 2.

Row 5: Ch 1, sc in each st across to last st, 2 sc in last st, turn (20).

Rows 6-9: Repeat rows 2 and 5 alternately, ending with 22 sc in last row.

Row 10: Ch 1, sc in each st across, turn.

Row 11: Ch 1, 2 sc in first st, sc in each st across, turn (23).

Row 12: Ch 1, sc in each st across, turn.

Rows 13-17: Repeat rows 11 and 12 alternately, ending with row 11 and 26 sc in last row.

Rows 18-21: Repeat row 11 (30).

Rows 22-25: Repeat rows 10 and 11 alternately, ending with 32 sc in last row.

Rows 26-27: Ch 1, sc in each st across, turn.

Row 28: Ch 1, sc first 2 sts tog, sc in each st across, turn (31).

Row 29: Ch 1, sc in each st across to last 2 sts, sc last 2 sts tog, turn (30).

Rows 30-36: Repeat rows 28 and 29 alternately, ending with row 28 and 23 sc.

Row 37: Ch 1, sc in each st across to last 4 sts, sc next 2 sts tog leaving remaining sts unworked, turn (20).

Row 38: Repeat row 28 (19).

Row 39: Repeat row 37 (16).

Row 40: Ch 3, 2 sc in 2nd ch from hook, sc in next ch, 2 sc in first st, sc in each st across, turn (20).

Row 41: Ch 1, sc in each st across to last st, 2 sc in last st, turn (21).

Row 42: Ch 3, 2 sc in 2nd ch from hook, sc in next ch, sc in each st across, turn (24).

Row 43: Ch 1, sc in each st across to last st, 2 sc in last st, turn (25).

Row 44: Ch 1, 2 sc in first st, sc in each st across, turn (26).

Rows 45-50: Repeat rows 43 and 44 alternately, ending with 32 sc in last row.

Rows 51-52: Ch 1, sc in each st across, turn.

Row 53: Ch 1, sc first 2 sts tog, sc in each st across, turn (31).

Rows 54-57: Repeat rows 52 and 53 alternately, ending with 29 sc in last row.

Rows 58-61: Repeat row 53 (25).

Row 62: Ch 1, sc in each st across, turn.

Row 63: Repeat row 53 (24).

Rows 64-68: Repeat rows 62 and 53 alternately, ending with row 62 and 22 sc in last row.

Row 69: Ch 1, sc in each st across to last 2 sts, sc last 2 sts tog, turn (21).

Row 70: Ch 1, sc first 2 sts tog, sc in each st across to last st, 2 sc in last st, turn.

Row 71: Repeat row 69 (20).

Rows 72-73: Repeat rows 70 and 71 (19).

Rows 74-76: Repeat row 70.

Row 77: Ch 1, sc in each st across, fasten off.

Cheek (make 2)

Row 1: With rose, ch 3, sl st in first ch to form ring, ch 1, 3 sc in ring, turn (3 sc).

Rows 2-3: Ch 1, 2 sc in each st across, turn (6, 12).

Row 4: Ch 1, sc in each of first 2 sts, 2 sc in next st, (sc in each of next 2 sts, 2 sc in next st) 2 times, sc in each of last 3 sts, turn (15).

Row 5: Ch 1, sc in each of first 3 sts, (2 sc in next st, sc in each of next 3 sts) across, turn (18).

Row 6: Ch 1, sc in first 4 sts, 2 sc in next

st, (sc in next 4 sts, 2 sc in next st) 2 times, sc in each of last 3 sts, turn (21).

Row 7: Ch 1, sc in first 4 sts, 2 sc in next st, (sc in next 5 sts, 2 sc in next st) 2 times, sc in last 4 sts; working in ends of rows, sc in first 4 rows, dc in each of next 3 rows, dc in ring, dc in each of next 3 rows, sc in last 4 rows, fasten off.

Eye (make 2)
Row 1: With black, ch 2, 4 sc in 2nd ch from hook, turn (4 sc).

Row 2: Ch 1, 2 sc in each st across, turn (8).

Row 3: Ch 1, sc in first st, 2 sc in next st, (sc in next st, 2 sc in next st) across; sl st in end of first 3 rows, sl st in opposite side of starting ch, sl st in end of last 3 rows, fasten off.

Left Eyebrow
Row 1: With white, ch 22, sc in 2nd ch from hook, sc in each ch across to last ch, 2 sc in last ch, turn (22 sc).

Rows 2-5: Ch 1, sc in each st across to last st, 2 sc in last st, turn, ending with 26 sc in last row. Front of row 2 is right side of work.

Row 6: Ch 1, sc first 2 sts tog, sc in each st across to last 2 sts, sc last 2 sts tog, turn (24).

Row 7: Ch 1, sc first 2 sts tog, sc in each st across, fasten off.

Right Eyebrow
Row 1: With white, ch 14, sc in 2nd ch from hook, sc in each ch across to last ch, 2 sc in last ch, turn (14 sc).

Row 2: Ch 1, 2 sc in first st, sc in each st across, turn (15). Front of row 2 is right side of work.

Row 3: Ch 1, 2 sc in first st, sc in each st across to last st, 2 sc in last st, turn (17).

Row 4: Repeat row 2 (18).

Row 5: Ch 1, sc in each st across to last st, 2 sc in last st, turn (19).

Row 6: Ch 2, sc in 2nd ch from hook, sc in each st across to last 2 sts, sc last 2 sts

tog, turn.

Row 7: Repeat row 5 (20).

Row 8: Ch 2, sc in 2nd ch from hook, sc in next 9 sts, sl st in next st leaving remaining sts unworked, turn (10).

Row 9: Ch 1, skip first sl st, sl st in next st, sc in each st across to last 2 sts, sc last 2 sts tog, turn (8).

Row 10: Ch 1, sc first 2 sts tog, sc in next 5 sts, sl st in last st, turn (6).

Row 11: Repeat row 9, fasten off.

Nose
Row 1: With red, ch 10, sc in 2nd ch from hook, (hdc in next ch, sc in next ch) across, turn (9 sts).

Row 2: Ch 1, (sc, hdc) in first st, sc in next st, (hdc in next st, sc in next st) across to last st, (hdc, sc) in last st, turn (11).

Row 3: Ch 2, (sc in next st, hdc in next st) across, turn.

Row 4: Ch 2, sc in same st, hdc in next st, (sc in next st, hdc in next st) across to last st, (sc, hdc) in last st, turn (13).

Row 5: Ch 1, sc in first st, (hdc in next st, sc in next st) across, turn.

Row 6: Ch 1, sc first 2 sts tog, hdc in next st, (sc in next st, hdc in next st) across to last 2 sts, sc last 2 sts tog, turn (11).

Row 7: Repeat row 3.

Row 8: Ch 2, skip next st, sc in next st, (hdc in next st, sc in next st) across to last 2 sts, hdc last 2 sts tog, turn (9).

Row 9: Repeat row 5.

Row 10: Ch 1, sc first 2 sts tog, hdc in next st, (sc in next st, hdc in next st) across, fasten off.

Face
Row 1: With beige, ch 11, sc in 2nd ch from hook, sc in each ch across, turn (10 sc).

Row 2: Ch 1, 2 sc in first st, sc in each st across, turn (11).

Row 3: Ch 1, sc in each st across, turn.

Row 4: Ch 1, 2 sc in first st, sc in each st across to last st, 2 sc in last st, turn (13).

Row 5: Repeat row 2 (14).

Continued on page 138

Portrait of Santa

Continued from page 137

Row 6: Repeat row 4 (16).

Row 7: Ch 6, sc in 2nd ch from hook, sc in next 4 chs, sc in each st across, turn (21).

Row 8: Ch 1, 2 sc in first st, sc in each st across to last 2 sts, sc last 2 sts tog, turn.

Row 9: Ch 1, sc first 2 sts tog, sc in each st across, turn (20).

Row 10: Repeat row 2 (21).

Row 11: Ch 1, sc in each st across, turn.

Row 12: Repeat row 2 (22).

Rows 13-33: Ch 1, sc in each st across, turn.

Row 34: Repeat row 9 (21).

Row 35: Ch 1, sc in each st across, turn.

Row 36: Repeat row 9 (20).

Row 37: Repeat row 2 (21).

Row 38: Ch 1, sc first 2 sts tog, sc in each st across to last st, 2 sc in last st, turn.

Row 39: Ch 1, sc in each st across, turn.

Row 40: Ch 1, sc first 2 sts tog, sc in next 12 sts, sc next 2 sts tog leaving remaining sts unworked, turn (14).

Row 41: Repeat row 9 (13).

Row 42: Ch 1, sc first 2 sts tog, sc in each st across to last 2 sts, sc last 2 sts tog, turn (11).

Row 43: Ch 1, sc in each st across, turn.

Row 44: Repeat row 9.

Row 45: Ch 1, sc in each st across, fasten off.

Beard

Row 1: With white mohair, ch 3, sc in 2nd ch from hook, 2 sc in last ch, turn (3 sc).

Row 2: Ch 4, sc in 2nd ch from hook, sc in each of next 2 chs, sc in each st across to last st, 2 sc in last st, turn (7).

Row 3: Ch 5, sc in 2nd ch from hook, sc in each of next 3 chs, sc in each st across to last st, 2 sc in last st, turn (12).

Rows 4-6: Ch 6, sc in 2nd ch from hook, sc in next 4 chs, sc in each st across to last

st, 2 sc in last st, turn (18, 24, 30).

Rows 7-9: Ch 3, sc in 2nd ch from hook, sc in next ch, sc in each st across to last st, 2 sc in last st, turn (33, 36, 39).

Row 10: Repeat row 2 (43).

Row 11: Repeat row 4 (49).

Rows 12-14: Repeat row 7 (52, 55, 58).

Rows 15-16: Ch 1, sc in each st across to last st, 2 sc in last st, turn (59, 60).

Rows 17-18: Repeat row 7 (63, 66).

Rows 19-29: Ch 1, 2 sc in first st, sc in each st across to last st, 2 sc in last st, turn (88).

Rows 30-40: Ch 1, sc in each st across, turn.

Rows 41-45: Ch 1, sc first 2 sts tog, sc in each st across to last 2 sts, sc last 2 sts tog, turn, ending with 78 sc in last row.

Row 46: For **first side,** ch 1, sc in first 23 sts, sc next 2 sts tog leaving remaining sts unworked, turn (24).

Row 47: Ch 1, sc first 2 sts tog, sc in each st across, turn (23).

Row 48: Ch 1, sc in each st across to last 2 sts, sc last 2 sts tog, turn (22).

Rows 49-52: Repeat rows 47 and 48 alternately, ending with 18 sc in last row.

Rows 53-54: Repeat row 41 (16, 14).

Rows 55-60: Ch 1, sc in each st across, turn.

Row 61: Ch 1, sc in each st across to last st, 2 sc in last st, turn (15).

Row 62: Ch 1, sc in each st across, turn.

Rows 63-64: Repeat rows 61 and 62 (16).

Row 65: Ch 7, sc in 2nd ch from hook, sc in next 5 chs, sc in each st across to last st, 2 sc in last st, turn (23).

Row 66: Ch 1, sc in each st across, turn.

Row 67: Repeat row 19 (25).

Row 68: Ch 1, sc in each st across, turn.

Row 69: Ch 1, sc in each st across to last st, 2 sc in last st, turn (26).

Row 70: Ch 1, sc in each st across to last 2 sts, sc last 2 sts tog, turn (25).

Rows 71-76: Repeat rows 69 and 70 alternately.

Row 77: Ch 1, sc in each st across to last 4 sts, sc next 2 sts tog leaving remaining sts

unworked, turn (22).

Row 78: Ch 1, sc in each st across, turn.

Rows 79-80: Ch 1, 2 sc in first st, sc in each st across, turn (23, 24).

Rows 81-82: Ch 1, sc in each st across, turn.

Row 83: Ch 1, sc in each st across to last 2 sts, sc last 2 sts tog, turn (23).

Row 84: Ch 1, sc first 2 sts tog, sc in each st across, turn (22).

Rows 85-88: Repeat rows 83 and 84 alternately, ending with 18 sc in last row.

Row 89: Ch 1, sc in each st across to last 4 sts, sc next 2 sts tog leaving remaining sts unworked, turn (15).

Row 90: Repeat row 84, **do not** turn, fasten off (14).

Row 46: For **center,** skip next 5 sts on row 45, join with sc in next st, sc in next 17 sts leaving remaining sts unworked, turn (18).

Rows 47-53: Ch 1, sc first 2 sts tog, sc in each st across to last 2 sts, sc last 2 sts tog, turn, ending with 4 sc in last row.

Rows 54-55: Ch 1, sc in each st across, turn.

Row 56: Ch 1, sc first 2 sts tog, sc last 2

sts tog, **do not** turn, fasten off (2).

Row 46: For **second side,** skip next 5 sts on row 45, join with sl st in next st, ch 1, sc same st and next st tog, sc in each st across, turn (24).

Row 47: Ch 1, sc in each st across to last 2 sts, sc last 2 sts tog, turn (23).

Row 48: Ch 1, sc first 2 sts tog, sc in each st across, turn (22).

Rows 49-52: Repeat rows 47 and 48 alternately, ending with 18 sc in last row.

Rows 53-54: Repeat row 41 (16, 14).

Rows 55-61: Ch 1, sc in each st across, turn.

Rows 62-91: Repeat rows 61-90 of first side.

Sew all pieces to Afghan as shown in photo.

Tassel (make 4)

For **each Tassel,** cut 50 strands green each 18" long, tie separate strand green tightly around middle of all strands; fold in half. Tie 10" strand around folded strands ¾" from fold, secure. Trim ends.

Tie one Tassel to each corner of Afghan.

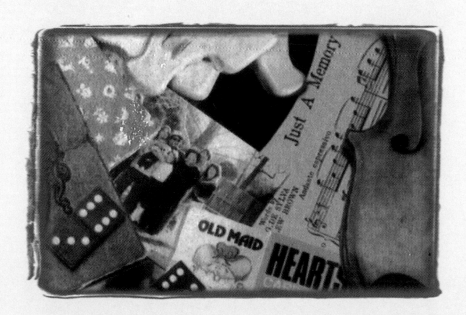

Bedroom Charm

Purple Passion

Relax and enjoy some restful reading time wrapped in the soft folds of this lusciously textured afghan that's as pretty as it is practical.

AFGHAN

Row 1: Ch 160, sc in 2nd ch from hook, sc in each ch across, turn (159 sc).

Row 2: Ch 3, dc in each st across, turn.

Row 3: Ch 1, sc in each of first 2 sts, *[tr in next st, (sc in next st, tr in next st) 2 times], sc in next 5 sts; repeat from * across to last 7 sts; repeat between [ ], sc in each of last 2 sts, turn.

Note: For **treble crochet front post stitch (tr fp** — *see fig. 7, page 158),* yo 2 times, insert hook from front to back around post of next st on row before last, yo, draw lp through, (yo, draw through 2 lps on hook) 3 times; skip next st on last row.

Row 4: Ch 3, (dc in next 7 sts, tr fp, dc in next st, tr fp) across to last 8 sts, dc in last 8 sts, turn.

Rows 5-182: Repeat rows 3 and 4 alternately.

Row 183: Ch 1, sc in each st across, turn, fasten off.

For **edging,** working in ends of rows across one long edge, with right side of work facing you, join with sc in first row, sc in each row across, fasten off.

Joining in last row, repeat edging on opposite edge.

Designed by Eleanor Albano-Miles *for Monsanto's Designs for America Program*

FINISHED SIZE
53" x 69".

MATERIALS
Worsted-weight yarn —
80 oz. lilac; I crochet hook or size needed to obtain gauge.

GAUGE
3 sts = 1"; 4 dc rows and 4 sc rows = 3".

SKILL LEVEL
Easy

Christmas Snowflake

Carry the holiday atmosphere into the bedroom with this exhilarating quilt-look afghan stitched in shades of winter white.

Designed by
Katherine Eng

FINISHED SIZE
43" x 65".

MATERIALS
Worsted-weight yarn —
48 oz. white and 7 oz.
off-white; tapestry
needle; H crochet
hook or size needed
to obtain gauge.

GAUGE
7 sts = 2". Each Block
is 7¾" square.

SKILL LEVEL
Average

BLOCK (make 40)

Rnd 1: With white, ch 6, sl st in first ch to form ring, ch 1, sc in ring, (ch 3, sc in ring) 7 times; **to join,** dc in first sc (8 ch sps).

Rnd 2: Ch 1, (sc, ch 3, sc) around joining dc, *ch 3, (sc, ch 3, sc) in next ch sp; repeat from * around, join as before (16 ch sps).

Note: For **shell,** (2 dc, ch 2, 2 dc) in next ch sp.

Rnd 3: Ch 1, sc around joining dc, shell in next ch sp, (sc in next ch sp, shell in next ch sp) around, join with sl st in first sc (8 sc, 8 shells).

Rnd 4: Ch 5, sc in ch sp of next shell, ch 2, (dc in next sc, ch 2, sc in ch sp of next shell, ch 2) around, join with sl st in 3rd ch of ch-5 (8 sc, 8 dc, 16 ch sps).

Rnd 5: Ch 1, sc in each st and 3 sc in each ch sp around, join with sl st in first sc (64 sc).

Rnd 6: Ch 2, *[dc in each of next 2 sts, tr in next st, (2 tr, ch 2, 2 tr) in next ch sp, tr in next st, dc in each of next 2 sts, hdc in each of next 2 sts, sc in next 5 sts], hdc in each of next 2 sts; repeat from * 2 more times; repeat between [ ], hdc in last st, join with sl st in top of ch-2 (19 sts between each corner ch sp, 4 ch sps).

Rnd 7: Ch 1, sc in each st around with (sc, ch 2, sc) in each corner ch sp, join, fasten off.

Rnd 8: Join off-white with sc in any corner ch sp, ch 2, sc in same sp, *[ch 1, skip next st, (sc in next st, ch 1, skip next st) across to next corner], (sc, ch 2, sc) in next corner ch sp; repeat from * 2 more times; repeat between [ ], join, fasten off.

Rnd 9: Join white with sc in any st, sc in each st and in each ch-1 sp around with (sc, ch 3, sc) in each corner ch sp, join, fasten off (25 sc between each corner ch-sp, 4 ch sps).

Holding Blocks wrong sides together, matching sts, with white, sew together through **back lps** in five rows of eight Blocks each.

BORDER

Rnd 1: With right side facing you, join white with sc in any corner ch-3 sp, ch 3, sc in same sp, sc in each st, sc in each ch sp on each side of seams and hdc in each seam around with (sc, ch 3, sc) in each corner ch sp, join with sl st in first sc (139 sc on each short end between corner ch sps, 223 sc on each long edge between corner ch sps, 4 ch-3 sps).

Rnd 2: Ch 1, sc in each st around with (sc, ch 3, sc) in each corner ch sp, join, **turn,** fasten off

Continued on page 154

Diamonds & Ripples

Dazzling stripes in a zig-zag pattern transform an ordinary room into a private sanctuary filled with livable elegance.

PANEL A (make 8)

Row 1: With variegated, ch 3, sc in 2nd ch from hook, sc in last ch, turn (2 sc).

Row 2: Ch 1, 2 sc in first st, sc in last st, turn (3). Front of row 2 is right side of work.

Rows 3-13: Ch 1, 2 sc in first st, sc in each st across, turn, ending with 14 sc in last row.

Rows 14-25: Ch 1, sc first 2 sts tog, sc in each st across, turn, ending with 2 sc in last row.

Rows 26-241: Repeat rows 2-25 consecutively. At end of last row, fasten off.

Border

Row 1: With right side of work facing you, working in ends of rows, join pink with sc in first row, evenly space 10 sc across to next point, (*3 sc in next point, evenly space 11 sc across* to next indentation, skip next row, evenly space 11 sc across to next point) 9 times; repeat between **, turn (250 sc).

Note: Work remaining rows in **back lps** only.

Row 2: Ch 1, sc first 2 sts tog, sc in next 10 sts, 3 sc in next st, (sc in next 11 sts, skip next 2 sts, sc in next 11 sts, 3 sc in next st) 9 times, sc in next 10 sts, sc last 2 sts tog, turn, fasten off.

Row 3: Join lavender with sl st in first st, ch 1, sc first 2 sts tog, sc in next 10 sts, 3 sc in next st, (sc in next 11 sts, skip next 2 sts, sc in next 11 sts, 3 sc in next st) 9 times, sc in next 10 sts, sc last 2 sts tog, turn.

Row 4: Repeat row 2.

Rows 5-6: With white, repeat rows 3 and 4.

Repeat on opposite edge of Panel.

PANEL B (make 7)

Row 1: With variegated, ch 15, sc in 2nd ch from hook, sc in each across, turn (14 sc).

Rows 2-13: Ch 1, sc first 2 sts tog, sc in each st across, turn, ending with 2 sc in last row. Front of row 2 is right side of work.

Rows 14-25: Ch 1, 2 sc in first st, sc in each st across, turn, ending with 14 sc in last row.

Rows 26-241: Repeat rows 2-25 consecutively. At end of last row, fasten off.

Border

Row 1: With right side of work facing you, working in ends of rows, join pink with sc in first row, evenly space 11 sc across to next indentation, skip next row, (evenly space 11 sc across to next point, 3 sc in next point, evenly space 11 sc across to next inden-

Continued on page 154

Designed by
Darla J. Fanton

FINISHED SIZE
49" x 78".

MATERIALS
Worsted-weight yarn —
29 oz. variegated,
15½ oz. each pink and
lavender, 12 oz. white;
G crochet hook or
size needed to
obtain gauge.

GAUGE
4 sc = 1";
5 sc rows = 1".

SKILL LEVEL
Average

Ruffles Galore

A feminine vision of pale blue and white, this extravagantly lacy design brings subtle character to milady's bedchamber.

FIRST STRIP

Notes: For **cluster (cl),** yo, insert hook in next ch or ch sp, yo, draw lp through, yo, draw through 2 lps on hook, yo, insert hook in same ch or ch sp, yo, draw lp through, yo, draw through 2 lps on hook, yo, draw through all 3 lps on hook.

For **shell,** (cl, ch 1, cl) in next ch sp.

Row 1: With lt. blue, ch 5, shell in 5th ch from hook, turn (1 ch-4, 1 shell).

Rows 2-63: Ch 4, shell in ch sp of next shell, turn. At end of last row, **do not** turn, fasten off.

Rnd 64: Working in ch sps and in ends of rows, join white with sc in beg ch-4 on last row, ch 3, 3 dc in next shell, ch 3, sc in bottom of next cl, *ch 3, (sc in next ch-4 sp, ch 3, sc in bottom of next cl, ch 3) across*, 3 dc in bottom of starting ch; repeat between **, join with sl st in first sc (128 ch-3 sps, 126 sc, 6 dc).

Rnd 65: Sl st in first ch sp, ch 1, 3 sc in same sp, *sc in next st, (sc, ch 1, sc) in next st, sc in next st*, 3 sc in next ch sp, (ch 1, 3 sc in next ch sp) 63 times; repeat between **, (3 sc in next ch sp, ch 1) 63 times, join, fasten off.

Note: For **long half double crochet (lhdc),** working over ch-1 sp on last rnd, yo, insert hook between bars of next sc (see illustration) on rnd before last, yo, draw up long lp, yo, draw through all 3 lps on hook.

Rnd 66: Join lt. blue with sc in 2nd st, ch 3, skip next st, *sc in next st, ch 3, skip next st, (sc, ch 2, sc) in next ch-1 sp, ch 3, skip next st, (sc in next st, ch 3, skip next st) 2 times*, (lhdc, ch 3, skip next st, sc in next st, ch 3, skip next st) 63 times; repeat between **, lhdc, ch 3, skip next st, (sc in next st, ch 3, skip next st, lhdc, ch 3, skip next st) 62 times, join, fasten off.

Rnd 67: Join white with sc in last ch sp, sc in next ch sp, ch 5, *sc in next ch sp, ch 3, (sc, ch 2, sc) in next ch sp, ch 3, sc in next ch sp, ch 5*, (sc in each of next 2 ch sps, ch 5) 64 times; repeat between **, (sc in each of next 2 ch sps, ch 5) 63 times, join, fasten off.

Rnd 68: Join lt. blue with sc in ch-2 sp at one end, ch 2, sc in same sp, *ch 3; working behind next ch sp, sc in next sc on rnd before last, ch 3; working in front of next ch sp on last rnd, sc in next sc on rnd before last, (ch 5; working in back of next ch sp on last rnd, sc in next lhdc on rnd before last, ch 5; working in front

Continued on page 155

Designed by Jennifer Christiansen Simcik

FINISHED SIZE
55" x 74½".

MATERIALS
Worsted-weight yarn — 35 oz. lt. blue and 29 oz. white; H crochet hook or size needed to obtain gauge.

GAUGE
1 shell = 1";
5 shell rows = 5½".

SKILL LEVEL
Challenging

Colonial Charm

As mellow as a fine antique, this quick-as-a-wink creation is the perfect addition to lend distinction to a well-used guest room.

STRIP (make 6)

Note: Use 3 strands same color held together throughout.

Row 1: With blue, ch 2, sc in 2nd ch from hook, turn (1 sc).

Rows 2-73: Ch 1, sc in sc, turn.

Notes: For **beginning shell (beg shell),** ch 3, (2 dc, ch 2, 3 dc) in same st or sp.

For **shell,** (3 dc, ch 2, 3 dc) in next st or ch sp.

Rnd 74: Working in sts and in ends of rows around outer edge, beg shell in st on last row, skip first row, dc in next 71 rows, skip last row, shell in starting ch, skip first row, dc in next 71 rows, skip last row, join with sl st in top of ch-3, fasten off (142 dc, 2 shells).

Rnd 75: Join white with sc in ch sp of any shell, ch 2, sc in same sp, *ch 1, skip next st, (sc, ch 1, sc) in next st, ch 1, skip next st, (sc in next st, ch 1, skip next st) 36 times, (sc, ch 1, sc) in next st, ch 1, skip next st*, (sc, ch 2, sc) in next ch sp; repeat between **, join with sl st in first sc, fasten off (84 sc, 84 ch sps).

Rnd 76: Join blue with sl st in ch-2 sp at one end of Strip, beg shell, *2 dc in next ch sp, (dc, ch 1, dc) in next ch sp, 2 dc in next 37 ch sps, (dc, ch 1, dc) in next ch sp, 2 dc in next ch sp*, shell in next ch sp; repeat between **, join with sl st in top of ch-3, fasten off.

Rnd 77: Join white with sc in ch sp of any shell, 2 sc in same sp, (sc in next 6 sts, 2 sc in next ch sp, sc in each st across to next ch sp, 2 sc in next ch sp, sc in next 6 sts), 3 sc in next ch sp; repeat between ( ), join with sl st in first sc, fasten off.

Holding Strips wrong sides together, matching sts, with two strands white held together, sew long edges together through **back lps** leaving 13 sts on each end unsewn.

TASSEL (make 16)

For each Tassel, cut 30 strands white each 12" long. Tie separate strand tightly around middle of all strands; fold strands in half. Tie 18" strand 1½" from top of fold; secure. Trim ends.

Tie one Tassel to each end of Strips.

Designed by Maggie Weldon *for Monsanto's Designs for America Program*

FINISHED SIZE
48" x 63"
not including Tassels.

MATERIALS
Worsted-weight yarn —
50½ oz. blue and 29½ oz. white; tapestry needle; Q hook or size needed to obtain gauge.

GAUGE
With 3 strands held together, 10 sts = 7"; 1 dc rnd and 1 sc rnd = 2¼".

SKILL LEVEL
Easy

Bunches o' Blossoms

Fill your personal hide-away with a refreshing bouquet of flirty posies you can crochet in a hurry and catnap on at your leisure.

Designed by
Maggie Weldon
*for Monsanto's
Designs for America
Program*

FINISHED SIZE
46½" x 65".

MATERIALS
Worsted-weight yarn —
50½ oz. black, 21 oz.
teal, 12½ oz. each
lt. berry and lt. blue;
tapestry needle;
Q hook or size needed
to obtain gauge.

GAUGE
Each Square is
6½" square.

SKILL LEVEL
Easy

SQUARE A (make 35)

Note: Use 3 strands same color held together throughout.

Rnd 1: With lt. blue, ch 3, sl st in first ch to form ring, ch 1, (sc, 2 tr) 4 times in ring, join with sl st in first sc, fasten off (8 tr, 4 sc).

Notes: For **beginning shell (beg shell),** ch 2, (2 hdc, ch 2, 3 hdc) in same st or sp.

For **shell,** (3 hdc, ch 2, 3 hdc) in next st or ch sp.

Rnd 2: Join teal with sl st in first sc, beg shell, shell in each sc around, join with sl st in top of ch-2, fasten off (4 shells).

Rnd 3: Join black with sl st in first ch sp, beg shell, 3 hdc in sp between last shell and next shell, (shell in next ch sp, 3 hdc in sp between last shell and next shell) around, join, fasten off.

SQUARE B (make 35)

Rnd 1: With lt. berry, repeat same rnd of Square A.

Rnds 2-3: Repeat same rnds of Square A.

Holding Squares wrong sides together, matching sts, starting with Square B in upper left-hand corner and alternating Squares A and B, with 2 strands black held together, sew together through **back lps** in seven rows of ten Squares each.

EDGING

Join black with sl st in any st, ch 3, dc in each st, in each ch sp on each side of seams and in each seam around with (dc, ch 1, dc, ch 1, dc, ch 1, dc) in each corner ch sp, join with sl st in top of ch-3, fasten off.

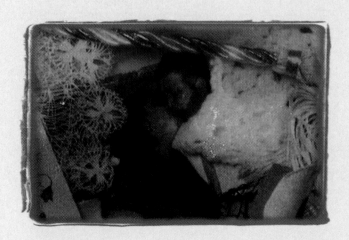

Christmas Snowflake

Continued from page 144

(141 sc on each short end between corner ch sps, 225 sc on each long edge between corner ch sps, 4 ch-3 sps).

Rnd 3: Join off-white with sc in any corner ch sp, ch 3, sc in same sp, *[ch 1, skip next st, (sc in next st, ch 1, skip next st) across to next corner], (sc, ch 3, sc) in next corner ch sp; repeat from * 2 more times; repeat between [ ], join, **turn.**

Rnd 4: Ch 1, sc in each st and in each ch-1 sp around with (sc, ch 3, sc) in each corner ch sp, join, fasten off (145 sc on each short end between corner ch sps, 229 sc on each long edge between corner ch sps, 4 ch-3 sps).

Note: For **beginning shell (beg shell),** ch 3, (dc, ch 2, 2 dc) in same sp.

Rnd 5: Join white with sl st in any corner ch sp, beg shell, *[sc in next st, (skip next 2 sts, shell in next st, skip next 2 sts, sc in next st) across to next corner], shell in next corner ch sp; repeat from * 2 more times; repeat between [ ], join with sl st in top of ch-3, **turn.**

Rnd 6: Ch 5, *[(sc in next shell, ch 2, dc in next sc, ch 2) across to next corner, (3 dc, ch 2, 3 dc) in next corner ch sp, ch 2], dc in next sc, ch 2; repeat from * 2 more times; repeat between [ ], join with sl st in 3rd ch of ch-5, **turn.**

Rnd 7: Ch 1, sc in each st and 2 sc in each ch sp around with (sc, ch 3, sc) in each corner ch sp, join with sl st in first sc.

Rnd 8: Ch 1, sc in first st, skip next 2 sts, shell in next st, skip next 2 sts, sc in next st, *shell in next corner ch sp, sc in next st, (skip next 2 sts, shell in next st, skip next 2 sts, sc in next st) across to next corner; repeat from * 2 more times, shell in next corner ch sp, (sc in next st, skip next 2 sts, shell in next st, skip next 2 sts) across, join.

Rnd 9: Ch 1, sc in first st, ch 3, (sc, ch 3, sc) in next shell, ch 3, sc in next sc, ch 3, [(sc, ch 3, sc, ch 5, sc, ch 3, sc) in next corner ch sp, ch 3, sc in next sc, *ch 3, (sc, ch 3, sc) in next shell, ch 3, sc in next sc, ch 3; repeat from * across to next corner]; repeat between [ ] 2 times, (sc, ch 3, sc, ch 5, sc, ch 3, sc) in next corner ch sp, ch 3, ◊sc in next sc, ch 3, (sc, ch 3, sc) in next shell, ch 3◊; repeat between ◊◊ across, join, fasten off.

Diamonds & Ripples

Continued from page 147

tation, skip next row) 9 times, evenly space 12 sc across, turn (249 sc).

Note: Work remaining rows in **back lps** only.

Row 2: Ch 1, sc in first 12 sts, skip next st, (*sc in next 11 sts, 3 sc in next st, sc in next 11 sts*, skip next 2 sts) 8 times; repeat between **, skip next st, sc in last 12 sts, turn, fasten off.

Row 3: Join lavender with sc in first st, sc in next 11 sts, skip next st, (*sc in next 11 sts, 3 sc in next st, sc in next 11 sts*, skip next 2 sts) 8 times; repeat between **, skip next st, sc in last 12 sts, turn.

Row 4: Repeat row 2.

Repeat on opposite edge of Panel.

Starting with Panel A, alternating Panels A and B, with white, sew Panels together through **back lps.**

EDGING

Row 1: Working across one long edge, join white with sc in end of first row, sc in end of each row and in each st across, turn.

Row 2: Ch 1, sc in each st across, turn, fasten off.

Repeat on opposite long edge.

Ruffles Galore

Continued from page 149

of next ch sp on last rnd, sc in next lhdc on rnd before last) 31 times, ch 5; working in back of next ch sp on last rnd, sc in next lhdc on rnd before last, ch 5; working in front of next ch sp on last rnd, sc in next sc on rnd before last, ch 3; working in back of next ch sp on last rnd, sc in next sc on rnd before last, ch 3*, (sc, ch 2, sc) in next ch-2 sp on last rnd; repeat between **, join, fasten off.

SECOND STRIP

Rows/Rnds 1-67: Repeat same rows/rnds of First Strip.

Note: For **joining ch-5 sp,** ch 2, drop lp from hook, insert hook from front to back through corresponding ch-5 sp on last Strip made, draw dropped lp through, ch 2.

Rnd 68: Join lt. blue with sc in ch-2 sp at one end, ch 2, sc in same sp, ch 3; working behind next ch sp, sc in next sc on rnd before last, ch 3; working in front of next ch sp on last rnd, sc in next sc on rnd before last, (ch 5; working in back of next ch sp on last rnd, sc in next lhdc on rnd before last, ch 5; working in front of next ch sp on last rnd, sc in next lhdc on rnd before last) 31 times, ch 5; working in back of next ch sp on last rnd, sc in next lhdc on rnd before last, ch 5; working in front of next ch sp on last rnd, sc in next sc on rnd before last, ch 3; working in back of next ch sp on last rnd, sc in next sc on rnd before last, ch 3, (sc, ch 2, sc) in next ch-2 sp on last rnd, ch 3; working behind next ch sp, sc in next sc on rnd before last, ch 3; working in front of next ch sp on last rnd, sc in next sc on rnd before last, (work joining ch sp; working in back of next ch sp on last rnd, sc in next lhdc on rnd before last, work joining ch sp; working in front of next ch sp on last rnd, sc in next lhdc on rnd before last) 31 times, work joining ch sp; working in back of next ch sp on last rnd, sc in next lhdc on rnd before last, work joining ch sp; working in front of next ch sp on last rnd, sc in next sc on rnd before last, ch 3; working in back of next ch sp on last rnd, sc in next sc on rnd before last, ch 3, join, fasten off.

Repeat Second Strip eight more times for a total of ten Strips.

Getting Started

Yarn & Hooks

Always use the weight of yarn specified in the pattern so you can be assured of achieving the proper gauge. It is best to purchase at least one extra skein of each color needed to allow for differences in tension and dyes.

The hook size stated in the pattern is to be used as a guide. Always work a swatch of an afghan's stitch pattern with the suggested hook size. If you find your gauge is smaller or larger than what is specified, choose a different size hook.

Gauge

Gauge is measured by counting the number of rows or stitches per inch. Each of the afghans featured in this book will have a gauge listed. Gauge for some small motifs or flowers is given as an overall measurement. Proper gauge must be attained for the afghan to come out the size stated, and to prevent ruffling and puckering.

Make a swatch about 4" square in the stitch indicated in the gauge section of the instructions.

Lay the swatch flat and measure the stitches. If you have more stitches per inch than specified in the pattern, your gauge is too tight and you need a larger hook. Fewer stitches per inch indicates a gauge that is too loose. In this case, choose a smaller hook size. Next, check the number of rows. If necessary, adjust your row gauge slightly by pulling the loops down a little tighter on your hook, or by pulling the loops up slightly to extend them.

Once you've attained the proper gauge, you're ready to start your afghan. Remember to check your gauge periodically to avoid problems later.

Pattern Repeat Symbols

Written crochet instructions typically include symbols such as parentheses, asterisks and brackets. In some patterns a diamond or bullet (dot), may be added.

( ) Parentheses enclose instructions which are to be worked again later or the number of times indicated after the parentheses. For example, "(2 dc in next st, skip next st) 5 times" means to follow the instructions within the parentheses a total of five times. If no number appears after the parentheses, you will be instructed when to repeat further into the pattern. Parentheses may also be used to enclose a group of stitches which should be worked in one space or stitch. For example, "(2 dc, ch 2, 2 dc) in next st" means to work all the stitches within the parentheses in the next stitch.

* Asterisks may be used alone or in pairs, usually in combination with parentheses. If used in pairs, the instructions enclosed within asterisks will be followed by instructions for repeating. These

---

SKILL LEVEL REQUIREMENTS:

Easy — Requires knowledge of basic skills only; great for beginners or anyone who wants quick results.

Average — Requires some experience; very comfortable for accomplished stitchers, yet suitable for beginners wishing to expand their abilities.

Advanced — Requires a high level of skill in all areas; average stitchers may find some areas of these patterns difficult, though still workable.

Challenging — Requires advance skills in both technique and comprehension, as well as a daring spirit; some areas may present difficulty for even the most accomplished stitchers.

repeat instructions may appear later in the pattern or immediately after the last asterisk. For example, "*Dc in next 4 sts, (2 dc, ch 2, 2 dc) in corner sp*, dc in next 4 sts; repeat between ** 2 more times" means to work through the instructions up to the word "repeat," then repeat only the instructions that are enclosed within the asterisks twice.

If used alone an asterisk marks the beginning of instructions which are to be repeated. Work through the instructions from the beginning, then repeat only the portion after the * up to the word "repeat"; then follow any remaining instructions. If a number of times is given, work through the instructions one time, repeat the number of times stated, then follow the remainder of the instructions.

[ ] Brackets, ◊ diamonds and • bullets are used in the same manner as asterisks. Follow the specific instructions given when repeating.

Finishing

Patterns that require assembly will suggest a tapestry needle in the materials. This should be a #16 or #18 blunt-tipped tapestry needle. When stitching pieces together, be careful to keep the seams flat so pieces do not pucker.

Hiding loose ends is never a fun task, but if done correctly, will keep your afghan looking great for years. Always leave 6-8" of yarn when beginning or ending. Thread the loose end into your tapestry needle and carefully weave through the back of several stitches. Then, weave in the opposite direction, going through different strands. Gently pull the end and clip, allowing the end to pull up under the stitches.

If your afghan needs blocking, a light steam pressing works well. Lay your afghan on a large table or on the floor, shaping and smoothing by hand as much as possible. Adjust your steam iron to the permanent press setting, then hold slightly above the stitches, allowing the steam to penetrate the yarn. Do not rest the iron on the afghan. Allow to dry completely.

For More Information

Sometimes even the most experienced needlecrafters can find themselves having trouble following instructions. If you have difficulty completing your project, write to:

Afghan Traditions Editors
The Needlecraft Shop
23 Old Pecan Road, Big Sandy, Texas 75755

Acknowledgments

Our sincerest thanks and appreciation goes to the following manufacturers for generously providing their product for use in the following projects:

Brunswick
Bunches o' Blossoms ....Windrush

Caron International
Circles, Checks & Squares ....Wintuk
Colonial Charm...Wintuk
Laura's Roses...Simply Soft
Purple Passion ....Dawn Sayelle
Ruffles Galore...Simply Soft

Coats & Clark
Christmas Snowflake ....Red Heart Super Saver
Jewels of Time ....Red Heart Super Saver
Lavender Fascination ....Red Heart Super Saver
Quilted Pastels.....................Red Heart Super Saver
Rosewood Elegance ....Paton's Canadiana
Woven Fisherman ....Red Heart Super Saver

Lion Brand
Grapevine Lace ....Jiffy
Stars in the Mist ....Jiffy

National Yarn Crafts
Sunlight & Shadows ....Natura Sayelle
Vanilla Delight ....Natura Sayelle
Velvet Morning ....Natura Sayelle

Spinrite
Diamonds & Ripples ....Bernat Softee
Touched by Color ....Bernat Berella "4"
Treble-Toned Shells ....Bernat Berella "4"

Stitching Artists
Susie Spier Maxfield......................Wish Upon a Star
Shirley Brown ....Laura's Roses
Ruffles Galore Woven Fisherman

Photography Locations & Special Help
Photography locations: James and Mary Barnet, Arp; Jim and Narlene Capel, Gardenside Bed and Breakfast, Mt. Pleasant; Phyliss Glazer, Winona; Kaun Kidwell, The Red Geranium, White Oak; Pat and Gary Jernigan, Arp; Rudy Belony, Big Sandy; A.C. Upright, Greggton Florist in Longview.
Props: Country Girl Antiques/Diana Taylor in Gladewater; Georgia's Plants in White Oak and Hawkins Florist in Hawkins.

Stitch Guide

BASIC STITCHES

 1 ### Front Loop (A)/Back Loop (B)
(front lp/back lp)

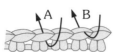

 2 ### Chain
(ch)

Yo, draw hook through lp.

 3 ### Slip Stitch
(sl st)

Insert hook in st, yo, draw through st and lp on hook.

 4 ### Single Crochet
(sc)

Insert hook in st (A), yo, draw lp through, yo, draw through both lps on hook (B).

 5 ### Half Double Crochet
(hdc)

Yo, insert hook in st (A), yo, draw lp through (B), yo, draw through all 3 lps on hook (C).

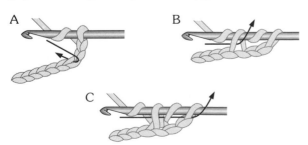

 **6** ### Double Crochet
(dc)

Yo, insert hook in st (A), yo, draw lp through (B), (yo, draw through 2 lps on hook) 2 times (C and D).

 7 ### Treble Crochet
(tr)

Yo 2 times, insert hook in st (A), yo, draw lp through (B), (yo, draw through 2 lps on hook) 3 times (C, D and E).

Standard Stitch Abbreviations

ch(s)	chain(s)
dc	double crochet
dtr	double treble crochet
hdc	half double crochet
lp(s)	loop(s)
rnd(s)	round(s)
sc	single crochet
sl st	slip stitch
sp(s)	space(s)
st(s)	stitch(es)
tog	together
tr	treble crochet
tr tr	triple treble crochet
yo	yarn over

8. Double Treble Crochet (dtr)

Yo 3 times, insert hook in st (A), yo, draw lp through (B), (yo, draw through 2 lps on hook) 4 times (C, D, E and F).

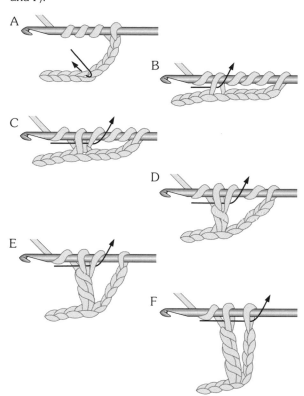

SPECIAL STITCHES

9. Front Post/Back Post Stitches (fp/bp)

Yo, insert hook from front to back (A) or back to front (B) around post of st on indicated row; complete as stated in pattern.

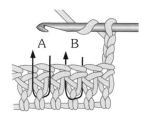

10. Reverse Single Crochet (reverse sc)

Working from left to right, insert hook in next st to the right (A), yo, draw through st, complete as sc (B).

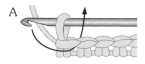

CHANGING COLORS

11. Single Crochet Color Change (sc color change)

Drop first color; yo with 2nd color, draw through last 2 lps of st.

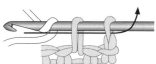

12. Double Crochet Color Change (dc color change)

Drop first color; yo with 2nd color, draw through last 2 lps of st.

DECREASING

13. Single Crochet next 2 stitches together (sc next 2 sts tog)

Draw up lp in each of next 2 sts, yo, draw through all 3 lps on hook.

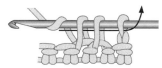

14. Half Double Crochet next 2 stitches together (hdc next 2 sts tog)

(Yo, insert hook in next st, yo, draw lp through) 2 times, yo, draw through all 5 lps on hook.

15. Double Crochet next 2 stitches together (dc next 2 sts tog)

(Yo, insert hook in next st, yo, draw lp through, yo, draw through 2 lps on hook) 2 times, yo, draw through all 3 lps on hook.

Index

A-B

Albano-Miles, Eleanor . .143
American Beauty 59
Blue Magic 36
Brooks, Dorris 89
Bubbles & Broomsticks .110
Bunches o' Blossoms . .152
Burgundy Expressions . .34

C-D

Cabled Lattice 64
Chamberlain, Lena 119
Champagne Lace 26
Christmas Snowflake . .144
Circles, Checks & Squares 74
Cloisonñe 33
Colonial Charm 151
Cranberry Frost 122
Diamonds & Ripples . . .147
Dzikowski, JoHanna 33

E-F

Eng, Katherine 11, 12,
. . . .47, 86, 90, 99, 144,
Etched Copper 69
Everson, Linda 107
Fanton, Darla J. . . .121, 147
Flight of Fancy 92
Flower Fantasy 56

G-I

Garen, Kathleen D. 67
Geometrix 67
Granny's Attic Window . .17
Grapevine Lace 86
Harshman, Rosetta 83
Heavenly Rainbows . . .109
Hetchler, Fran 19, 85
Homespun Harmony . .119

J-L

Jewels of Time 125
LaRoche, Jeannine 69
Laura's Roses 30
Lavender Fascination . . .47
Lazy Afternoon 19
Lilac Time 80

M-N

Maier, Roberta 103
Marlin, Francine . .126, 131
Maxfield, Sandra Miller . .48
Maxfield, Susie Spier . . .70
McKee, Pamela J. 100
Medley in Blue 83
Monsanto's Designs for
America Program . . .40,
. .74, 132, 143, 151, 152
Myers, Dorothy C. 20
Nagy, Maria 64
New Baby on the Block 103

P-R

Panda Parade 107
Patchwork Flowers 8
Party Gingham 112
Petite Medallions 39
Plaited Ripple 70
Portrait of Santa 131
Purple Passion 143
Quilted Pastels 99
Rosewood Elegance 89
Roy, Barbara 53
Ruffles Galore 149

S-T

Scalloped Squares 20
Semonis, Sara 109
Shepherd, Shep . .36, 50, 56
Shifting Sapphires 85

Simcik, Jennifer
Christiansen .30, 73, 149
Simpson, Rhonda . . .59, 92
Smith, Ann E. 74
Smith, Sandra 39, 110
Southwest Echoes 126
Spring Lattice 50
Stars in the Mist 40
Stevens, Rena V. 26
Stuart, Kathleen 17
Sunflowers 53
Sunlight & Shadows 12
Tender Innocence 100
Thomm, Lisa 122
Touched by Color 121
Treble-Toned Shells . . .132

V-W

Vanilla Delight 90
Velvet Morning 11
Watkins, Vicki M. 112
Watson, Daisy . .34, 80, 125
Weldon, Maggie 40,
. . . . .132, 151, 152
Wilhelm, Mary 8
Wish Upon a Star 48
Woven Fisherman 73